GREAT
BUSINESS
TEAMS

GREAT BUSINESS TEAMS

Cracking the Code for Standout Performance

Howard M. Guttman

WILEY

John Wiley & Sons, Inc.

Published by John Wiley & Sons, Inc., Hoboken, New Jersey.
Published simultaneously in Canada.

For general information on our other products and services or for technical support, please contact our Customer Care Department within the United States at (800) 762-2974, outside the United States at (317) 572-3993 or fax (317) 572-4002.

Wiley also publishes its books in a variety of electronic formats. Some content that appears in print may not be available in electronic books. For more information about Wiley products, visit our web site at www.wiley.com.

Library of Congress Cataloging-in-Publication Data:

Guttman, Howard M.
    Great business teams : cracking the code for standout performance / Howard M. Guttman.
        p.   cm.
    Includes bibliographical references and index.
        ISBN 978-0-470-12243-3 (cloth)
        1. Teams in the workplace—Management.   2. Employee empowerment.   3. Senior leadership teams.   4. Communication in organizations.   5. Group decision making.
    I. Title.
    HD66.G88   2008
    658.4'022–dc22   2008002743

Printed in the United States of America

10   9   8   7   6   5   4   3   2   1

"Most discussions of decision making assume that only senior executives make decisions or that only senior executives' decisions matter. This is a dangerous mistake."

—Peter Drucker

This book is dedicated to our many clients, who recognize that the high-performance, horizontal organization, with its focus on distributive decision making, is the best way to create a sustainable business model.

Contents

Preface

This past summer, with postseason play hanging in the balance, the starting pitcher for the Philadelphia Phillies had a bad-arm day. In five-plus innings, he allowed six hits, four runs, two walks, and three homers. His reaction? "For the most part," he commented, "I was happy with the way I threw the ball."[1]

This pitcher, at least on that day, was not a high-performing player. He failed to deliver in a crucial situation. Even more significantly, he failed to accept accountability for his subpar performance.

The leaders you will encounter in this book are a very different breed. They and the "players" on their teams are connected by a common thread: a set of qualities and behaviors that makes them stand apart as high performers.

Each of them has overcome a significant business challenge to deliver impressive results in clutch situations. In the process, they have put in place a radically new high-performance, horizontal organizational model. They have also learned to think differently about themselves, their colleagues, and their organizations, which has had significant implications on how they lead, make decisions, accept accountability, and confront issues—and one another—to become great players, on great teams, in great organizations.

After more than 25 years of consulting with senior executive teams throughout the world, we have discovered that there is a code for standout performance: one that applies to every organization, regardless of size, type, or industry affiliation. Cracking that code does not guarantee a perfect outcome every time you engage in competitive play. But, by changing your game, you will acquire a sustained competitive advantage and the ability to excel in a very difficult marketplace. Make the change and you will likely join the ranks of the great leaders and teams you will meet in the pages that follow.

Great Business Teams: Cracking the Code for Standout Performance is based on our work with, and in-depth interviews of, 39 senior executives from 25 organizations. It also includes insights from a number of onsite observations of actual teams, as they traveled along the road to high performance. The fact that these executives and their organizations have allowed us to "go public" is a tribute to one quality of high-performance players that we did not mention in the book: They are generous in spirit and want others to profit from their experience.

Note

1. Zolecki, Todd. "Eaton Gets Roughed Up." *The Philadelphia Inquirer,* September 12, 2007, E1.

Acknowledgments

I am indebted to the clients of Guttman Development Strategies, Inc. who allowed us to document their experiences and go on the record with the findings. For sharing their insights, they merit heartfelt thanks from me and, undoubtedly, from everyone who turns this page to discover what great business teams are, how to create them, and how to deploy them to achieve standout performance.

I also want to thank the GDS consultants who have been catalysts for change in client companies. Working within these companies, they have demonstrated a unique ability to go where they need to go in order to produce measurable results.

Thanks go to Larry Alexander and Matt Holt of John Wiley & Sons for the confidence they have had in this undertaking.

The core team of Jackie Guttman—chief operating officer of GDS and possessor of an editorial eagle eye—and Dale Corey and Peter Tobia of Market Access, our literary agency, proved to be a great business team. Their dedication, focus, and commitment made the creation of this book a much easier task than I had expected.

1

Cracking the High-Performance Code

The Great, the Bad, and the Consequences

Even to sharp-eyed sports commentator John Feinstein, the golfers who compete in the National Qualifying Tournament, or Q School, are indistinguishable from those who make it to the pro tour. They have picture-perfect swings, and they can drive a golf ball 300 yards.

What distinguishes the Tiger Woods and Phil Michelsons from those who never graduate from the Q School? According to Feinstein, it is the ability to perform supremely well under the pressure of a high-stakes tournament and, most tellingly, within the five feet of space separating the golf ball from the cup.

The ability to consistently excel under pressure is not just the hallmark of great golfers; it also separates great business teams from the merely good ones. Great teams rise time and again to overcome great challenges. It is a remarkable achievement—in some ways more impressive than what the pros in tournament golf accomplish, considering that it takes not just one star performer, but a team of stars, to pull it off.

At 5 AM on November 26, 2006, a thousand people stood in line in Chicago, waiting for Best Buy to open its doors—and they were the latecomers. In Philadelphia, despite wind, rain, and 40-degree temperatures, lines at the King of Prussia Mall began forming at 3 AM. In Murray, Utah, 15,000 shoppers poured into the Fashion Place Mall just after midnight. According to newspaper accounts, entire shelves of merchandise were cleared in minutes, and retail stores were as packed as nightclubs.

It is called "Black Friday" for a reason. Each year, retailers count on this day to move their balance sheets from red to black. On Black Friday 2006, over $622 million was spent every minute. Every second that a retail cash register stayed silent on that day was a major loss. At Chico's, a women's clothing chain with more than 500 stores, traffic was slow. The company had planned a nationwide marketing event for Black Friday, with easels in front of each store advertising "40% off already marked-down merchandise." But the customers just were not buying. Store managers were calling the company's Florida headquarters looking for direction—and fast.

On Black Friday speed and the ability to turn on a dime are next to godliness.

At 11 AM, the company's head of marketing picked up the phone and called his store leadership team, asking, "Is our current marketing approach working? Is that easel out front getting shoppers into our stores instead of Talbot's or Ann Taylor?" "No," he was told by the team leader, "most of the store managers report that it's not working." After a quick huddle to appraise the situation, Marketing swung into action, calling the stores with a new strategy: bring in the easels and the markdowns, and replace them with front-of-the store tables displaying accessories. New signs would read, "Buy one accessory, get the second one 50% off." "Great!" came the response, and the 500 outlets and their teams moved swiftly to execution.

"We changed our nationwide marketing approach before noon," says Chico's CEO, Scott Edmonds. "That change delivered strong same-store sales. It saved Black Friday for Chico's, and it happened in the snap of a finger."

In a second organization, Novartis Oncology, a number of key teams were about to take on a major challenge that would test their ability to win under pressure.

In 2003, executives at Novartis Oncology awoke to a potentially disastrous development. The company's marquee product, Glivec—until then the only drug available to treat a very rare and deadly form of leukemia—was being threatened by the introduction of a new product from a rival pharmaceutical company. The new product was projected by analysts to grab 20 to 30% of the market once it gained approval.

With Glivec representing nearly half of Novartis Oncology's revenue, implications were grim. The outlook was not much better for the company's critically ill customers, who might be switched to the new drug prematurely, before doctors knew its long-term survival rates and side effects. Nothing less than the lives of its customers and Novartis Oncology's number-one revenue driver were at stake.

CEO David Epstein swiftly called on his division vice presidents to put together action teams capable of "gaming" business scenarios. Each team represented a different aspect of the market: Glivec team; competitor team; and a team representing Tasigna, a potential second-generation leukemia drug that was in Novartis's R&D pipeline.

They ran no-holds-barred simulations that played out how the competition might position itself, how Novartis might respond, and what the market might look like in five years. No option or potential outcome was left unexplored. "The teams had the chance to beat each other up under different scenarios," Epstein says. "Then they developed strategies to help them win in those scenarios."

And they did win.

As a result of the games, the teams realized that Tasigna would have to be brought to market much more quickly than scheduled and that personnel shifts were needed. Tasigna development was accelerated, becoming one of the fastest developments of a pharmaceutical product—from discovery to filing—in history.

Since Glivec was effective in about 90% of patients, and trying to displace Glivec could create an opening for the new competition, Novartis Oncology needed a unique strategy. It boldly positioned the newer drug as a "more selective" second-line therapy to be prescribed for patients whose illness has progressed. It further identified that the competitor's product might make a good third-line therapy, due to its multiple mechanisms of action.

This team-built strategy allowed Novartis Oncology to integrate two of its products while sidelining the competition. When the competitor's drug came on line it took a meager 6% of the market in its first 18 months, leaving Novartis Oncology's bottom line—and its patients—healthy.

In yet another case, a team in Latin America was forced to reinvent itself—or suffer the consequences.

When Brian Camastral took over Mars Inc.'s Latin American division in 2005, the 3,000-associate operation had been consistently underperforming. Many millions of dollars had been invested in the region, with no return.

The division's yearly financials were a constant surprise. Smaller units would consistently report healthy numbers 10 months in a row, then—with 60 days left on the calendar—reveal $10 to 20 million shortfalls.

Leadership was practically nonexistent. In two years, the division had gone through four presidents. Camastral was the fifth. The entire executive level of the organization was rife with churn, as star associates fled faster than they could be promoted. Not surprisingly, any notion of team cohesion had long since evaporated.

As a result, Mars Inc. Latin America was starving in a land of plenty. The organization's growth was stagnant amidst a population of over 560 million potential customers. Brian Camastral knew the stakes and took charge. It was time to win.

Camastral's top agenda: make his organization flat, fast, and team driven. To do so, Camastral divided the organization's three lumbering operational segments—South America, Mexico, and the Caribbean—into a sleeker, more manageable geography. Brazil, for instance, became an independent unit, as did the Southern Cone, comprised of Argentina, Chile, Uruguay, and Paraguay. Out of the original three units, Camastral and his team created seven focused and nimble teams.

Accountability became the go word. Camastral engaged team members one on one, making them keenly aware of where responsibilities began, ended, and overlapped.

Results were measurable and incentives were rich. It was not long before each unit wanted to be a winning team and a division wide *esprit de corps* prevailed.

Turnover became a nonissue, and more than 70% of management-level openings have been filled from within the company.

In just 12 months, the division began experiencing double-digit growth. The annual budget surprises became nothing but a memory as the agile teams met all earnings targets and blew away bottom-line expectations.

"We have created so many business opportunities in the last two years that we don't have the capacity to take advantage of them all," says Camastral. It is the kind of dilemma that every organization longs to face, and one that Camastral and his team will be dealing with for some time to come.

Meanwhile, at Applied Biosystems, a life sciences company, senior executives struggled to regain the health and vitality of their organization.

When Catherine Burzik became president of Applied Biosystems (AB), she knew she faced stiff challenges. The company she was about to lead had been stagnant for several years, with little revenue growth and falling stock prices. Worse yet, it seemed that the company's R&D glory days were behind it. Despite significant R&D expense, there were few new products in the pipeline. Those that had been brought to market were not making the expected ROI. Both Wall Street and AB employees had lost confidence in the company.

What the company lacked in commercial performance, it made up for in a noble mission. AB aimed at nothing short of improving the human condition. And it backed up its mission with impressive past scientific accomplishment. AB created every instrument used in the sequencing of the human genome. AB's systems enable researchers around the globe to uncover the basic laws of nature and to further their understanding of human disease. AB's forensic DNA kits enable police to catch criminals and exonerate the innocent.

But in 2004, when Burzik assumed the top position, she saw that AB— which had enabled unparalleled scientific research for nearly 25 years—was about to flat line. Past glory would not be enough to secure the company's future.

Burzik's mission: work with her executive team of 15 vice presidents to craft and execute a strategy to get the company moving again. She quickly moved to push decision making down from her office to the team—a significant shift, given the command-and-control style of leadership in the company. A Division Presidents' Council, made up of the presidents of AB's four global business divisions, became the forum in which to raise and resolve tactical issues common to all. An Executive Strategy Team was created to identify and evaluate possible mergers and acquisitions. A third subteam, run by the vice president of finance, was charged with keeping a close watch on the numbers. A fourth focused strictly on R&D.

Speedy decision making and implementation began to replace bottlenecks and impasses. The new decentralized team structure, the minimalist approach to decision making—fewer decision makers per issue and more decision making per capita—and greater individual accountability freed up Burzik to pursue the next round of competitive advantage.

As a result of these changes, business accelerated. AB's stock price nearly doubled, as did its market cap. Revenue began to grow and the bottom line has seen double-digit performance. After several years of no acquisitions, two significant ones were successfully completed.

"Now AB's teams confront and deconstruct business challenges with confidence," says Burzik. "They know they have the tools to win."

Contrast the responses of these four great teams with those at a number of high-profile private and public organizations that have made the news in recent years. For example:

- **K-Mart's inability to fend off competition from Wal-Mart.** Ignoring the handwriting on the wall for over a decade, Big K was always a step or two behind. Now, the once-number-one discount retailer in the world ranks a distant third, behind both Wal-Mart and Target.
- **Merck's attempts to squelch reports of safety concerns about Vioxx**, which were revealed by the *Wall Street Journal*. Amid a storm of criticism and ill-will, the company was forced to withdraw the drug, got hit with dozens of lawsuits, and saw its stock price plunge 27%.
- **Mitsubishi executives' cover-up of defects in 580,000 vehicles.** The revelation of the attempt to avoid recalls knocked $200 million off the price DaimlerChrysler paid for a stake in the Japanese automaker,

destroyed consumer confidence in the brand, and cost hundreds of thousands of yen in government fines.

- **FEMA's botched response to Hurricane Katrina:** lucrative, no-bid contracts handed out to politically connected firms; families housed in high-priced hotels while rows of government trailers sat empty; $1 billion squandered on fraudulent assistance. And, several years later, a large portion of the U. S. Gulf Coast still uninhabitable.
- **The failed DaimlerChrysler merger.** German management refused to fully integrate the two companies for fear of tarnishing the Mercedes brand, and CEO Jurgen Schrempp admitted publicly that he had never intended the deal to be a "merger of equals."[1] Employees and investors who felt betrayed left the company and dumped their stock, and the ailing and emasculated Chrysler Corporation ended up on the auction block.
- **Airbus's delivery of only one new behemoth plane,** the A380, in 2007, down from the 25 originally promised. Once expected to revolutionize air travel and leave top rival Boeing in the dust, the aircraft was two years behind schedule and $2 billion over budget. And, while Airbus still has only half the A380 orders it needs to break even, Boeing is churning out its new, souped-up 747—which has almost the same capacity as the A380.

There are no Q Schools in the world of hypercompetitive global business. Losing teams, especially those at the top of an organization, do not often get to play another round.

What Makes the Standouts Stand Apart?

Whether a CEO and top-management team charged with setting strategy; a plant manager and shop-floor personnel committed to getting a defect-free product out the door; or a cross-functional, global project team dedicated to a worldwide product launch, teams are today's locus of power, responsibility, and action.

Great teams make great organizations. Period. Good and mediocre teams make good and mediocre organizations. They meet deadlines; they stay within budget; they maintain the *status quo*. But they do not push the envelope. They do not typically reach for performance breakthroughs. It is unlikely they will set the world on fire. And, over the long haul, they will take you out of the game.

Inept teams, especially at senior levels, can do irreparable damage to a company's brand, product line, customer relationships, and share value. Even those organizations with deep pockets in these areas can teeter and crash. Just ask former employees of Arthur Andersen, PanAm, Texas Instruments, Westinghouse, Zenith, and many of the other companies that have fallen off the radar screen.

For over 25 years, we have been helping clients create great business teams and great business organizations. Great business teams are not necessarily top management teams. They can be found in the boardroom or on the plant floor. But, when a top executive team is great, it has the authority and positional charisma to set in motion a chain reaction that can transform the performance of teams throughout the organization.

What makes great business teams stand apart? And how can they be replicated throughout an organization? We have thought long and hard about these questions. We searched for the answers not in theory but in practice—in the experiences of our clients. The organizations we have worked with were under the gun to produce results. Not unreasonably, they pressed us to do the same, and to do so rapidly. Hunch, trial-and-error testing, and retesting trumped conceptual finesse. We looked for distinctions between what worked and what did not. This process led us to a set of core attributes that have helped unlock the performance code of great teams. *Great business teams are high-performing, horizontal teams that operate as fully aligned entities to achieve increasingly higher levels of results.*

No matter where in the organization they are housed, how many or what level employees they include, what task they have been charged with, or how long their tenure, *great business teams share five characteristics:*

1. Great Business Teams are Led by High-Performance Leaders Who . . .

. . . **create a "burning platform" for fundamental change.** High-performance leaders are in a hurry. They are impatient with the *status quo.* Their sense of urgency is driven by a compelling business challenge—a threat or an opportunity—that must be met or exploited. In a skilled leader's hands, that challenge becomes a "burning platform"—an energizing principle—

for enrolling others to overcome the presenting challenge and, in so doing, to address deeper issues related to how employees view themselves, their roles, and their relationships; how work gets done; and what it means to be a contributor. In other words, high-performance leaders convert the challenge into a business case for radically and permanently changing an organization and the behavior of those who work for it.

In Burzik's case, the challenge was to jack up revenue growth and share-value. Camastral's challenge was to jump-start a stagnant organization. At Novartis Oncology, Epstein faced a significant competitive threat to his organization's most important growth driver. And Edmonds' ambitious plans to grow Chico's would have amounted to little more than pipe dreams, without the vim and vigor exhibited by high-performing teams such as the one that saved the day on Black Friday.

. . . are visionaries and architects. Many business leaders are visionaries. But a high-performance leader holds out a unique vision. To overcome the immediate challenge and those that lie ahead, high-performance leaders like Burzik, Camastral, Edmonds, Epstein, and the other senior executives you will meet in the pages that follow have scuttled the traditional hierarchical organizational model and replaced it with a "flat," horizontal one. As Burzik puts it, "Most organizations function on a hub-and-spoke model, with decisions radiating from a central base of power. They're not built for high performance and speed."

But a leader needs to be more than a visionary. The question is: Can you lead your team and organization down from the mountaintop? Given the demands placed on today's organizations, visions need to be operationalized, which is a unique strength of high-performance leaders. They have an architect's flair: able to see the whole game—the blueprint, not just the vision—for creating a great business organization. And they know how to inspire in others the desire to make that blueprint a reality.

. . . know they cannot do it alone. High-performance leaders are not necessarily charismatic or heroic, though, as we shall see later on, it takes guts and grit to be one. They are team players. Their notion of teamwork is not driven by ideological notions of "shared decision making" or "engagement," but by strictly utilitarian considerations. High-performance leaders believe they are more powerful and effective—and their organizations create greater value—in the presence of high-performing teams that function horizontally.

Over the last 10 years, Cathy Burzik, like other high-performance leaders, has learned that the only way to accelerate performance is by going horizontal: empowering teams throughout the organization to make the decisions formerly made at the top. In her words, "It enables you to multiply yourself."

Like great architects, high-performance leaders surround themselves with people who can bring their blueprints to life. They do not put the hammer to the wood, but they need people who can. They remain riveted on answering such questions as: Who are the players, and what competencies must we develop or acquire to create a high-performance organization? What role do I play in bringing this about?

As Epstein puts it, "I ask senior executives, 'Do you want to live in a world where you are constantly putting out fires and solving problems? Or would you rather live in a world where the rest of the organization is working to solve its own problems, where most issues are solved at levels below yours, and where you spend your time focusing on where you want to drive the business?'"

In Scott Edmonds' case, he knew that for Chico's to survive and succeed in the dog-eat-dog world of women's retailing, where styles and taste can change on a whim, the company had to change the way it operated. Moving to a horizontal structure, based on great business teams, would allow Chico's to act quickly and decisively. As Edmonds sees it, a horizontal organization is "ruled by high-performance teams with real decision-making clout and accountability for results, rather than by committees that pass decisions up to the next level or toss them over the wall to the nearest silo."

. . . build authentic relationships. To great leaders, *authenticity* has a special meaning: holding up a mirror to players to reflect, in real time, how well they measure up to the requirements of a high-performance environment. And being a *relationship builder* also has a special meaning. It does not involve being a "people person," with "natural interpersonal skills." Rather, it is about building trust so that the entire team can openly discuss, assess, and confront one another on actual performance in order to raise the bar. This relationship-building process begins with the leader posing tough questions in *five key areas:*

- What is the business strategy, and how committed are we to achieving it?
- What key operational goals flow from the strategy, and how do we make sure these goals drive day-to-day decision making?
- Are we clear on roles and accountabilities?
- What protocols, or ground rules, will we play by as a team?

■ Will our business relationships and interdependencies be built on candor and transparency?

In the process of raising these questions with team members and in the give-and-take search for answers, effective leaders lay the groundwork for a solid, performance-oriented set of relationships. What emerges is a fully aligned and engaged team of players who think and act like a mini board of directors.

. . . **model the behaviors they expect from their team.** Leaders exercise a kind of gravitational pull on their team. Their behavior sets the performance "should be" for others. It can spawn an army of imitators.

Outside Scott Edmonds' office, a sign is posted that reads, in language that everyone at Chico's understands, "I practice HPTs (high-performing teams)." The sign reminds visitors that they are about to enter a high-performance zone, and it also reminds Edmonds to practice what he preaches: authenticity, transparency, receiving and delivering candid feedback, holding himself and others accountable, and an uncompromising focus on business results.

. . . **redefine the fundamentals of leadership.** High-performance leaders tend not to focus on restructuring, reorganizing, or reengineering—at least not as a going-in priority for changing how their organizations get results. If you buy into the proposition that Burzik, Camastral, Edmonds, Epstein, and other leaders of great teams have advanced, then the leader's first task is to change mindsets, beginning with his or her own. This type of leader commands without commanding. He or she has the strength to put aside ego and not merely encourage team members to make decisions and produce results—but actually hold them accountable for doing so.

Power—who gets what and how?—is a fundamental principle of social life. Within high-performing organizations, power flows not so much up and down as across the organization, and it is *distributed* to players and teams that have been aligned. It's a major departure from tradition, to say the least.

In redefining their own role, high-performance leaders see the net advantage of letting go, which frees them from many of the more onerous aspects of the traditional leadership model, ranging from playing Solomon to acting as enforcer. "As Chico's grew more complex," recounts Edmonds, "we began to operate in silos within a centralized decision-making structure. It was driving me crazy," he says, thinking back to the days before Chico's began creating teams on every level. "I felt as though, if it didn't change, they wouldn't be able to pay me enough to put up with it. Life is too short to be a referee or a dad trying to keep peace among all the siblings in the family."

2. Members of Great Business Teams are Us-Directed Leaders

On a team that aspires to greatness, the leader is not the only one who must undergo a change in mindset. Team members must also do so, or the model does not work. "When I turn around," says Epstein, "what I want to see is leaders, not followers"; and, in Camastral's view, "a high-performing team is not a leaderless team, but a team of leaders."

For a team to make this transition, every member must look deeply at him- or herself to answer the basic question: What does it mean to be a player in this organization and on this team? If the answer is anything short of "It's about *us* winning," then the team is not even close to becoming great. While it is unrealistic to expect complete abandonment of functional thinking, high-performance players have learned to subordinate functional self-interest to winning for the team. Their compass points are oriented more toward moving the business forward and more toward "us" than toward "me" and "my function."

The most unique characteristic of a great team involves a mindset change that is difficult to bring about. It centers on one word: *accountability*. When it comes to holding others accountable, we are programmed to think vertically, not horizontally, and downward rather than upward. Members of great business teams have broken free of these constraints. They think of themselves as accountable not only for their own performance, but for that of their colleagues—even those who do not report to them. In this new model, the head of IT would feel perfectly comfortable and, in fact, obligated to question actions by the head of marketing that may be putting a new product launch at risk. The controller would have no qualms about asking the director of Human Resources (HR) to explain the ROI of a new training program.

On a great business team, no one's—not even the leader's—performance is exempt from scrutiny and feedback. When he set out to create a great business team, Brian Camastral knew this would go along with the territory. "The general managers and staff now call me immediately when they think I am off target," he recounts. "After the team decided that the

Brazilian business should be broken up into more focused pieces, they told me I was moving too slowly on execution. I had to speed up the process."

As *us*-directed leaders, team members are unafraid to go where others fear to tread. If there is an uncomfortable issue—the proverbial dead elephant's head in the room—whether it be an underperforming peer, a strategic issue, an operational glitch, a potential problem, or a missed opportunity, they confront it with a bias toward action.

Burzik points to an incident that illustrates how far her top executive team at Applied Biosystems traveled in its ability to step up and confront an issue:

> I discovered that several members of my team would appear to agree to decisions in team meetings but then go back to their organizations to drive different, nonaligned agendas. Often, this misalignment was apparent to subsets of the team, but not to the entire team—and the subsets failed to bring the issues to everyone's attention. The lack of alignment eventually became obvious to the entire team during a number of strategic business reviews. The situation eventually crescendoed, and I had to take action on several team members. The experience proved to be a major moment of truth in the evolution of the team. They had been hoping that I would recognize the problem, so they waited and didn't take action. They finally came to realize that it wasn't just *my* business to run; it was *theirs* as well.

3. Great Business Teams Play by Protocols

A great business team leaves nothing to chance. The more structured its way of working together, the less likelihood of misunderstandings, conflict, or costly delays and bottlenecks. Counterintuitive as it may seem, the fastest-moving, most innovative teams we know spend a fair amount of time crafting hard-and-fast protocols and living by them. One important set of protocols relates to decision making.

High-performance leaders no longer make all the decisions. They may, in fact, make very few. While that is all to the good in terms of the speed of decision making, it also muddies the once-clear waters. Who will now be responsible for which decisions? Will they be expected to make the decision unilaterally, or will they be required to get input from others? Does the team expect them to actually make the decision or to present a recommendation?

Ambiguity kills effective decision making. It also wastes precious time. Great business teams are crystal clear about what decisions they need to make, who will make them, and how. They tend to follow a carefully laid-out process: identifying the decisions that have to be made, identifying subteams to make them, assigning accountability for getting closure, and selecting a decision-making mode—unilateral, consultative, or by consensus.

One of the first things Burzik and her team at Applied Biosystems did was put in place formal protocols for decision making. "All strategic-level decisions were made by the full team," explains Burzik, "but lower-level decisions were made by subteams. We operated like a board of directors that has committees to which it delegates fact finding and decision making." The results speak for themselves.

Interpersonal conflict can be a greater obstacle to high performance than lack of resources, shifting priorities, or unclear goals. The latter can usually be resolved by creative thinking, but the former are impervious to logic. Some team members may be holding onto "stories" about their colleagues or holding grudges against them. Others may be overly aggressive, abrasive, and generally unpleasant. Or they may be poor team players—undependable, uncommunicative, out for themselves.

The great business team also agrees on protocols for interpersonal behavior, especially in dealing with conflict. Straight-up rules such as "no triangulation or enlistment of third parties," "resolve it or let it go," "don't accuse in absentia," and "no hands from the grave, or seconding-guessing decisions" can eliminate much of the unresolved conflict that paralyzes teams and keeps them from moving to a higher level of performance.

Those who aren't willing to shift their behavior don't last long. Those who are willing but skill deficient are given the training and coaching they need to modify their personal style.

4. Great Business Teams Continually Raise the Performance Bar

No matter how much it achieves, a great business team is never satisfied. The *status quo* is always on trial. As Ken Bloom, CEO of INTTRA, Inc., puts it, "If you think you are done, you are *done.*"

It used to be that organizations enjoyed periods of homeostasis, hit a speed bump, then went through another period of homeostasis before the next round of change. Now, there are only speed bumps. In a world in which pressure never ends, teams must always be looking ahead, anticipating the next bump and being totally prepared when it comes.

On a great business team, self-monitoring, self-evaluation, continuous improvement, and raising the performance bar are the norm. Rick Rizzo is a high-performance leader who, like the four others cited at the beginning of this chapter, has helped to create great business teams in a number of major pharmaceutical companies. "At one time," says Rizzo of his current team, "they were like an outfielder trying to never drop a ball. They were always trying to play it safe, talking down targets and low-balling goals. They never tried to make the dramatic catch—where you take the leap and may or may not catch the ball. If you get it, it's a big win; but if you drop it, it's a big failure."

The "play it safe" mindset evaporated completely as, under Rizzo's guidance, his group evolved into a great business team. They began setting stretch goals for themselves and, after attaining them, kept raising the bar. "Now, one of the attributes of the team is constructive dissatisfaction," continues Rizzo. "The team believes that, no matter how well it has done, it could have done better." Rizzo and his team always hold a year-end celebration of their success, and he never misses the chance to remind them of this. "Imagine how much better we could have done if we had not missed that opportunity or done thus and so, I point out. And other members of the team have started doing the same. Winning and exceeding expectations have become contagious."

5. Great Business Teams Have A Supportive Performance Management System

Whether your aim is to create a single great business team or an organization made up of great teams on every level, the shift is not a merely a structural, but a profoundly cultural, one.

A team on which the members have the power and authority of leaders, on which they themselves create and adhere to protocols for decision making and interpersonal behavior, on which goals are upwardly moving targets, and on which everyone acts like an owner of the business is far more than a new concept to most people: It flies in the face of much of what they have experienced.

In order to effect permanent behavior change, a team's performance management system must support the new expectations. Team and individual goals have to be crystal clear; the necessary technical and interpersonal skills have to be provided; performance has to be monitored; and feedback has to be timely and well thought out.

As we have seen, many of the requirements for serving on a great business team—accepting new levels of responsibility, holding one's peers and leaders accountable, acting as a director or owner rather than an employee, changing one's interpersonal style—force individuals far out of their comfort zones. Unless there are positive consequences for staying there—and negative ones for retreating—most people will quickly revert to old, safe ways of behaving. That is why great business teams only flourish when there are positive consequences for embracing team values and negative ones for flouting them.

"Skin in the game is crucial: the compensation system must provide positive consequences—including one of the best motivators—pay for performance," observes Leigh Ann Errico, an experienced executive coach and a seasoned hand at creating great business teams. "Sometimes you have to hit people right in the pocketbook," explains Errico. "In my experience, successful companies use performance management and compensation systems that look at both the hard facts—performance results—and leadership qualities—demonstration of company values or behavioral beliefs. If someone is not partnering well or trying to take all the credit for results, that person is not going to see the same rewards as someone who achieves performance results *and* is a pleasure to work with. And it really makes people change."

End Thought

History, Arnold Toynbee reminds us, is an unfolding process driven by a series of challenges and responses. The fortunes of nation states, business teams—and even golf games—stand or fall on the outcome of this dynamic process. Every organization and every team within it face challenges as they go about the tasks of solving problems and making decisions. Some teams just seem to take those challenges in stride, move quickly to resolution, and triumph over them. They then either move on to the next set of challenges, or, if the team is issue specific and temporary, members disband, justifiably proud of "mission accomplished." These teams enable their organization to endure as great companies, able to ride the crosscurrents in lean times and to reach for the stars in upturns.

To gain a thorough understanding of the "right stuff" of great teams, we will take a serious look into the key elements of great business teams that we have only touched on briefly in this chapter. In the chapters that follow, we will introduce you to a wide variety of teams and their leaders. Some have earned the label "great"; some are in the last stages of their journey to greatness; others have just started on the path. You will hear, in their own words, the stories of leaders and team members who have undergone personal transformations—and challenges—en route to high performance. You will see how ground rules, or protocols, for decision making and interpersonal behavior have kept many teams on track during their journey forward. We will discuss how typical teams continue to raise the bar, deal with the inevitable backsliding, and create a performance management system that helps sustain the new paradigm.

You will also have an opportunity to be a fly on the wall in some actual team-alignment sessions and meetings in which critical business and personal issues surfaced and were dealt with in real time. It will be an opportunity to witness how great teams play under pressure. Join us as we examine the making of great business teams and organizations.

Note

1. "Novel Insights into the Foundering Daimler-Chrysler Merger," *Knowledge@Emory,* June 05, 2002.

2

The New High-Performance Leader

Within Australia's fast-moving, competitive dairy industry, consumers have become more and more sophisticated, with ever-increasing wants and needs. In 2004, the industry was also witnessing dairy production declining, international farm gate milk prices skyrocketing to historic highs, and record global fuel costs.

That same year, Robert Gordon took over as CEO and managing director of Dairy Farmers, an Australia-based milk and value-added dairy company. He knew that his new assignment would not be a cakewalk.

Added to the hostile external atmosphere, the company's operating expenses were unsustainable. Financially, the company was not performing at capacity. There was unnecessary product proliferation and too much complexity. Organizationally, the company was largely siloed. Each function operated independently and was run by a general manager, sometimes competing with other functions for resources. Bottom line: It was time for radical change.

Leadership Imperative: Develop and Drive the Horizontal Vision

Gordon knew that beyond charting a new strategic framework for the business, the situation also called for rethinking the way in which his organization operated. He avoided the temptation to slip into organizational-chart tampering and reengineering modes. His first task was to think through what kind of organization would best enable Dairy Farmers of Australia to meet both its near-term challenges and those further over the horizon. "As I reviewed our situation," he reflected, "I was convinced that our best bet—indeed, our *only* bet—was to go horizontal."

Gordon was very clear about what he meant by going horizontal: "From my vantage, a horizontal organization means moving to an organization in which everyone operates according to a clearly defined set of decision-making protocols, where people understand what they are accountable for and then own the results. It means moving to an action-and results-driven workforce at every level—not one that waits around for instructions or trips over functional boundaries. It means giving employees the opportunity and skills to decide who needs to be involved in solving problems and making decisions, dividing responsibilities, then stepping aside to allow people to implement."

For Gordon and his team, the horizontal vision converted into an increase in organizational brainpower and performance muscle, from top to bottom. It upped speed to market, provided greater ownership of results, put the focus on the business and its customers, and reduced "hang time" for decisions. As Gordon relates, "The silos have been replaced by cross-functional business teams for each of our categories. Each team is accountable for the profitability of its category and operates fairly autonomously. They report back to the executive team periodically; they bring us into the loop when they have significant resource-allocation issues or need additional substantive funding. Otherwise, they are responsible for executing the strategy that we set together, and so far they're doing a fine job."

Three years later, Dairy Farmers has seen a dramatic turnaround. It has become significantly leaner: reducing its product portfolio by more than one third, closing 4 of 15 sites and 17 distribution depots, and divesting noncore businesses. The new lean, horizontal organization has chalked up a number of significant successes:

- It finished the 2007 year having replaced more than 15% of its total revenues in commodities with value-added branded sales.
- Time to market for new products was reduced significantly, resulting in Dairy Farmers winning the "New Product of the Year" award from the largest retailer in Australia.
- The company exited 2007 leading the growth rate in every retail market in which it participates and consequently improving market share in every category.
- It is now recognized by the leading financial press as a true fast-moving consumer goods business, not just a dairy cooperative.
- Following the rebuilding phase of the turn-around, staff turnover dropped significantly. In 2007, only one person left Marketing—only to return three months later because her new employer's culture was a disappointment after that of Dairy Farmers.

> "People can only deal with a certain amount of change at one time. It's highly variable from one person to another. You are putting people out of their comfort zone. It's a challenge to strike the right balance between getting them to change enough to make a difference and not making so many changes that they become paralyzed."
>
> —*Frank Verwiel, CEO*
> *Axcan Pharma*

Moving the organizational mountain in a radically different, horizontal direction is not easy, regardless of benefit. Fear of change and widespread initiative fatigue make the *status quo* very seductive. When Paul Michaels became president of Mars Incorporated in 2004, he knew that the company needed to achieve far greater growth and financial return. But he faced internal organizational challenges every bit as daunting as those he faced in the marketplace. The top team at Mars was siloed and replete with unspoken agendas. Members did not see the benefit of working as a team; they were only concerned with the success of their own region. There was some infighting, but mostly people just left one another alone.

Like Gordon, Michaels believed that the high-performance, horizontal model represented the best bet for the future. To drive his vision though his organization, he first created a "burning platform" for the change, which centered on business issues; he then shrewdly hooked his vision into Mars's core values. He explains:

> Mars has five guiding principles, one of which is efficiency, and high-performing teams are by far the most efficient way of operating. Without going through the process of creating high-performing teams, you may eventually get similar results, but it will take much longer, and you will make a lot of mistakes along the way. By using this process, teams quickly begin having authentic conversations, in real time: dealing with issues and not dancing around them. You see the impact quickly; people either step up or opt out. It becomes very evident where your issues are, who your players are, what you need to do to change the shape of the business. This model can speed up progress in these areas by years.

Michaels had been creating great business teams, within a horizontal organizational setting, for years. His colleagues were well aware that in previous positions at Mars he had moved brand teams and the Americas team to the high-performance, horizontal model. He had willingly given those teams more responsibility and power, so his new team knew he was coming from a place of respect for company values—and a solid track record of results.

Past experience had taught Michaels that functional thinking and hidden agendas are classic behaviors exhibited by nonhigh-performing teams. More than a "burning platform" was needed to counteract old habits and the natural tendency toward stand-pattism. Michaels' solution was to take his team through an "alignment"—an essential step in the transformation process to great business teams. This is where the leader/visionary evolves into the leader/architect.

Alignment is one of those buzz words that come loaded with baggage. To some it conjures up a mechanistic world: Alignment is what mechanics do to an automobile when the steering is out of whack. But alignment also evokes images of living organisms, as when a chiropractor aligns the body, readjusting the skeletal system to restore it to better balance and integration.

The alignment of teams and organizations has more to do with the human side of the term than with its mechanistic counterpart. Teams and the organizations they are part of are, after all, collective enterprises created by human beings to achieve results. When an organization is properly aligned, its parts move in sync to achieve results. There is a straight line of sight that goes from the organization's strategy to its customers. Scarce human, financial, and capital resources are deployed along that line of sight, so value gets created and added quickly, consistently, and cost effectively. This makes the aligned organization fiercely competitive and an ultimate high-performance entity. And you cannot have an aligned organization without aligned teams.

For an organization to raise its level of performance every team, on every level, must be a great team. That is to say, it must be aligned, or in sync, in *five key areas:*

1. business strategy
2. business deliverables coming from the strategy
3. roles and responsibilities at individual and business unit or functional levels
4. protocols, or ground rules, for decision making and conflict resolution
5. business/interpersonal relationships and interdependencies

The alignment process is the foundation for building those performance-based, leader–player relationships that characterize the high-performance teams described in Chapter 1. A team alignment is an opportunity for collective deep-think and reevaluation and for the leader and his or her team to establish the blueprint for high performance.

In Michaels' case, his team spent two intensive days in heated discussions about what they needed to accomplish, who was responsible for what, and who had the authority to make which decisions. They called one another out on unacceptable interpersonal behavior: failure to share information, lack of follow-through, riding roughshod over others, unilateral decision making, backbiting, and subterfuge. Michaels made it clear that he expected to be treated like every other member of the team. He wanted direct feedback and insisted on being held accountable for commitments and results. By the end of the two days, Michaels' team was on its way to becoming great.

Michaels believes that, as painful as some of the encounters were, the alignment served to quickly enroll the team in his vision. Some managers immediately went back and aligned their own team after the top team was aligned; others were more reticent but eventually saw the value of replicating the team model within their operation. A few people opted out: They were not equipped to play in the new environment.

Michaels had relatively little difficulty getting his senior team to buy into his vision of a horizontal organization made up of empowered teams. His direct reports understood the business case for growth and profitability. They also understood—if not before the alignment, then certainly after it—why he felt that going horizontal was the best way forward. But enrolling executives at the regional levels was more challenging. Michaels believes that this was because the regions were inwardly focused and concerned with day-to-day operations rather than longer-term business issues. A corporate "burning platform" is not always a hot seller regionally. The members of Michaels' team set about opening up a dialog with their direct reports around issues such as whether or not their area was growing in share, how profitable it was, what the future was likely to hold, and so on. The next logical step: Suggest a high-performance, horizontal solution. Now that Michaels' team sees the power of working horizontally, they are passing the torch to colleagues. Their goal: a great organization, made up of great teams, on every level.

Leadership Imperative: Create the Right Mindset

Playing at high-performance levels within a horizontal organization represents a radical departure from the norm. Those involved in the early transition stage often feel like strangers working in a strange land. The horizontal, flat organization and all it represents imply new expectations, rules, and ways of showing up as competent. Ultimately, it requires change at the deepest personal level—both on the part of the leader and his or her team. This is why high-performance leaders set about to address the second leadership imperative: creating the right collective mindset, one that hinges on high leader–player candor and willingness to accept a fundamental shift in the notion of accountability.

Being Candid

Whenever we work with a team that wants to raise the bar, we begin by asking each player to describe the collective mindset of the team as it currently exists:

- From "wary, closed, with hidden agendas," to "candid, open, relaxed, easy to speak your mind," how would you rate the working atmosphere within the team?
- From "no tolerance for confrontation; conflicts suppressed," to "tensions surfaced, confronted, and resolved," how are conflicts within the team handled?

Teams that are wary and closed, that suppress conflict rather than tackle it head-on, never achieve greatness. They tend not to take risks and to become inwardly directed. It is tough to focus on the market when you are looking suspiciously over your shoulder at competitor colleagues.

On a great business team, candor is king. If you have a point of view, you are free to express it. If there is conflict, you can resolve it without the usual game-playing. If you have feedback, you can give it, provided it is depersonalized and fact based. The objective is to move up performance and results. As Ken Bloom, CEO of INTTRA, describes it, "Great team members articulate feelings they have about issues, even when it makes them uncomfortable. Great team members know how to be candid and how to be receptive." Energy that formerly went into one-upmanship or subterfuge is rechanneled into positive action.

This change in mindset is a drastic and difficult one for most of us, conditioned as we are to hold back and bite our tongue, believing that discretion is the better part of valor and that "telling it like it is" is risky business.

Candor requires leaders to walk the talk. Team members must be open with one another, but first their leader has to be open and straightforward with them. A leader who brooks no disagreement can hardly expect others to encourage open dialogue. Leaders who ask for honesty must prove that they really want it—even if it is directed at them. They do this most convincingly by listening to critique of their own performance and acting on it, by changing behavior that the team tells them is unacceptable, by not cutting off dissenters or denigrating their opinions, by not

> "My greatest challenge was to become comfortable getting feedback from my team. I liked the idea of giving the leader feedback until I became the leader. When it was my turn, I worried that it would be difficult to take. In fact, it wasn't."
>
> —*Patrick Parenty, SVP General Manager, Redken Fifth Avenue*

pulling rank when it is time to make a decision. As Chuck Nesbit, executive vice president and COO of Chico's FAS, Inc., puts it, "If a lieutenant in Iraq doesn't have the courage to ride the Humvee down the road, he can't expect his troops to do it."

Candor takes thick skin. As chief learning officer for Mars Inc., Jon Shepherd is part of the global people and organization (HR) team. One of the meetings in which that team took part included a review of the team's answers to the questions, "How would you rate your leader's performance, and what does he need to do differently to improve it?" Shepherd believes that the team's leader demonstrated real bravery in the way he handled the feedback. "Our team is a very mixed group," he explains, "so the comments were all over the map. Some people wanted more direction and clarity, more structure; others were critical of the leader's tendency to solve their problems for them. Our leader sat through the long session—over an hour and a half—and listened to each person. He didn't try to explain or excuse himself; he didn't try to provide solutions. He just absorbed it." The leader then led a follow-up session in which he and the group identified actions they could take together to address each concern. "Hearing these things for the first time must shake you up and raise doubts about your abilities," adds Shepherd, "but our leader never got rattled or became defensive. He exhibited skill—and bravery."

And speaking of bravery and thick skin, Chico's President and CEO, Scott Edmonds, recently exhibited his fair share of both when he received some pretty tough feedback from his team. He had spearheaded the acquisition of Fitigues, a small (nine-store) specialty clothing chain. It became his pet project and he was soon devoting a great deal of time and energy to it. He did not realize that his emotional commitment outweighed his business sense until the members of his team called him on it. They told him, point blank, that the acquisition had become his blind spot and was draining his time away from core business issues. Their input enabled him to regain his perspective. He assessed Fitigues' performance objectively and closed the business. Members of Edmonds' team took note. Now, they not only do not hesitate to give their leader undiluted feedback, but they are just as honest with one another.

Larry Allgaier, CEO of Novartis's Global OTC business, believes that one of the best ways a leader can role-model candor is by owning up to his or her mistakes in front of the team. Unlike old-school leaders who carefully maintain the fiction of their infallibility, Allgaier openly admits misjudgments and turns them into learning experiences. He recounts his problems recruiting a global head of product supply. The position was empty when Allgaier became CEO, and within six months he filled it with a candidate of his own choice. The person was not a good fit for the job and quit in less than a year. Allgaier once again filled the job and, although the individual was highly qualified and was interviewed by other members of the lead team, the person lacked the cultural agility to make things happen with the rigor, depth, and speed required, and once again it was not a good fit. Allgaier decided to use the case as a learning opportunity for himself and his team. He held an candid three-hour debriefing with his lead team, beginning with his explaining what he felt he had missed in the two previous candidates. The team went deep, hammering out the real requirements of the job and proposing new ways to structure the role for enhanced speed of execution and organizational effectiveness the next time around. It took nine months to find the right person, but the third time around it worked out beautifully.

Allgaier encourages his team to follow his example. "I tell them that I want the bad news first, and no matter how bad it is I don't beat them up for it. The right type of players have high accountability for their work, and they already feel worse about their mistake than you can make them feel. We focus on what we can learn from the mistake and how we can correct it as soon as possible."

Accentuating Accountability

Vertical accountability is typical within a hub-and-spoke, functionally oriented organization. Executives, managers, and supervisors are driven by results—their own and those expected from subordinates. Rewards follow this vertical trajectory, with income and advancement tied to success in "my end" of the business.

The horizontal organization turns vertical accountability on its side. While individual and functional achievement are important, horizontal accountability puts equal emphasis on cross functional, peer-to-peer accountability, as well as peer-to-leader accountability. It sets up profoundly different performance expectations and approaches to rewards. Great team members know that doing their own job well is necessary but insufficient. Their peers—and the leader—must also operate at the highest performance level—and it is up to them to hold both accountable for doing so.

> "I had led large hierarchical organizations both in the U.S. and abroad, but here I faced a new challenge of leading a cross-divisional team with a disparate set of priorities and distinct agendas. I knew I needed to lead in a new way, and I knew my leadership style needed to evolve."
>
> —David H. Greenberg, SVP HR, L'Oréal USA

Great team leaders know that for horizontal accountability to take hold, they must role-model desired behaviors. They must deliver the message loud and clear: It is not only permissible, but expected, for team members to hold the leader accountable for business results, for observing agreed-upon protocols, and for interpersonal behavior.

Chico's Edmonds recounts how, six or seven months after a new member was added to his team, it became apparent that the individual was not delivering the needed results. The team was waiting for Edmonds to terminate him. Edmonds admits that he was "thinking too much from the heart and not enough from the head," so he dragged his feet for a while—until a couple of team members came into his office and shut the door. They told him that the team expected him to do something about this person and to do it quickly. Edmonds immediately stepped up and accepted accountability. He acknowledged that they were right, shook their hands, and said he was committed to taking swift action. He told them not to let him off the hook. Two days later he terminated the executive.

How often have you heard a CEO willingly submit to being held accountable by those who report to him or her? If you operate within a traditional hierarchical structure, chances are it has not been often—if ever.

Edmonds' role-modeling of accountability has paid off. In 2007, Chico's first-quarter business results were off plan, and things had not improved much by the end of May. His senior vice presidents (SVPs)—the second tier of his management team—did not wait around for permission to act; turning around poor performance was everyone's responsibility. Edmonds got a phone call from some of the SVPs saying, "As owners of the business we want to submit a plan to you and the EVPs to deal with the situation." Several days later, they presented the plan, which was on point and adopted with only minor modifications.

Paul Michaels is another high-performance leader with a demonstrated willingness to be held accountable. In Mars Inc.'s global business, there have been instances when someone in a particular region was underperforming.

Individual members of Michaels' team—his CFO, in one case—have taken it upon themselves to address the problem and resolve it directly with the overseas party. And, when staff in the regions had concerns about their managers, they used to report them to Michaels and expect him to deal with it. They have now graduated to telling Michaels about their concerns only after they have already initiated a conversation with the manager.

Larry Allgaier has a slightly different approach. Knowing how difficult it is for people to deliver negative feedback to "the boss," he has devised a way to make it easier. "If I have even an inkling that something is troubling someone," he explains, "I initiate a conversation that makes it easy for them to give me the feedback. For example, I called our general manager in France and said, 'I don't think I'm as connected with the European GMs as I need to be. What do you think?'" Knowing he had "permission" to deliver honest feedback, the GM did not hold back. His response: "You're right, Larry. I understand that the developing markets may need you more this year, but we would like to see you in our countries more often." Allgaier is convinced that he would not have gotten this feedback if he had not intentionally opened the door. He asks his team members to do the same thing with their own teams. Allgaier believes that, "Getting good feedback, honest and timely, is one of the hardest things for any executive because of the natural fear in the system. You have to really disarm people if you want the truth, and the faster you can get the truth, the faster you can apply the learning to yourself and your business."

Horizontal accountability flies in the face of vertical intuition, which is why the CEO's role in bringing about this mindset change is so crucial. When the leader and his or her top team model player-to-leader and player-to-player accountability for the rest of the organization, it extends to teams everywhere. Explains Ken Bloom, "If I don't do something I have promised, any member of my team can come to me and ask, 'Why aren't you honoring your agreement?' Everyone in the company knows it, and it gives them license to do the same."

In the next chapter, we will discuss in depth the challenge of getting peers to hold peers accountable, but there is one cardinal rule that always applies: It starts with the leader.

Mindset Change: Playing For Real

Not everyone is ready, willing, and able to embrace the mindset changes required to operate on a horizontal, great business team. A lot of "stuff" can get in the way: for example, holding on to a "story" that says, "If you show all your cards, someone else will win"; complacency; fear of having weaknesses exposed; and discomfort with the accountability requirement.

> "My biggest personal challenge was letting go. Sharing responsibility for success and failure is a two-way street. The team has to be willing to shoulder responsibility, and the leader has to be willing to give it to them. It requires trust and a leap of faith, but it's the only way leaders can do the job they're paid to do: think strategically."
>
> —Kenneth Bloom; President and CEO, INTTRA, Inc.

While, as we shall see in the next chapter, members of great business teams share responsibility with their leader for dealing with underperforming peers, the leader plays a critical role. The high-performance leaders we know have an up-or-out approach: Those who cannot adapt and thrive should take their game elsewhere. It is the ultimate in playing it for real.

One chief executive we know recalls that, in a healthcare organization he once worked for, he was persuaded to fill the position of finance director with an internal transfer who was highly recommended by several people. What these people neglected to mention was that the person had previously been passed over for the position of CFO. It soon became apparent that a great deal of resentment was still simmering under the surface. The new CFO craved center stage and had an unrealistic view of his capabilities. His colleagues had to tiptoe around him when providing feedback, and he never could see the point of horizontal accountability. The executive went to great lengths to salvage his new hire, from developing a closer personal relationship with him to nonjudgmental listening to asking his colleagues on the team to step into the breach and provide coaching. Nothing worked, and after several meltdowns during executive team meetings, it was time for this executive to move on. Reflecting back on the situation, the executive says, "You can only work at something for so long before you must say, 'This person has to go.' If you are not philosophically on the same page, or if you cannot convince a team member to be authentic, follow the protocols, and perform at the same level as colleagues, it's an unhealthy relationship. The team expends too much energy on the dysfunctional relationship when it should be working on business issues and winning over consumers and customers."

In this chief executive's view, the leader owes it to the rest of the team to make sure that everyone shares the high-performance mindset. "The team deserves people who are pulling for the whole team and not for themselves," he insists. "A great team member is someone who gives more than he or she takes."

Leadership Imperative: Provide the Right Skills

You cannot create a high-performing team by mindset alone. Everyone—including the leader—needs the right skills to play and win. Working horizontally is something of an unnatural act, given most people's experience working hierarchically. This creates a third leadership imperative: Ensure that everyone in the organization not only wants to but *can* contribute. To do so requires a specific menu of skills, such as influencing, active listening, assertion, giving and receiving feedback, conflict management, decision making, and leadership.

The great leaders with whom we have worked are shrewd students of human motivation. They know that the usual "butts in seats" approach to skills transfer typically does not have much impact. Learners have to be motivated, and one way to do so is to identify gaps in each player's skill repertoire and then create a sense of urgency to close them. To the extent that this comes about through a process of self-discovery on the learner's part, so much the better, but it also helps to have a leader and team members who assist in the process.

Think of the initial alignment session as a learning-by-doing exercise and a terrific crucible for revealing gaps. In working to answer the five questions that form the basis of alignment, the leader and team members grapple, publicly and often for the first time, with issues related to how they show up, day in and day out, as they make decisions, solve problems, and lead. As the team wades into areas related to protocols and business relationships, individuals are forced to look around at one another—and inwardly at themselves—to assess: Who is aggressive? Who is not assertive? Whose behavior is balanced? Who plays interdependently? Who confronts issues? Who is results focused?

Awareness aside, the discussion around these questions provides a rudimentary first step in practicing some of the core skills of high-performance players. The end result is often a great awakening about the distance the team leader and members will have to travel to take their performance to a new and higher level. And this sets up a compelling case for acquiring the needed skills.

Great leaders immediately develop an action plan to close skill gaps. They typically take a three-pronged approach:

1. formal skill-development workshops scheduled immediately after the alignment and pegged to the specific needs of team members
2. the ongoing search for opportunities to apply the skills
3. individual coaching, as needed

For example, Joe Pieroni, president and CEO of Daiichi Sankyo Inc., made sure that he and his team went through an influencing skills workshop soon after the alignment session. Prior to the workshop, a difference of opinion had arisen between two departments. Legal wanted to handle field-compliance issues itself, whereas HR felt that this was its own domain. Despite their best efforts, the issue remained unresolved. Pieroni realized that this contentious situation was a perfect venue in which to apply the newly acquired skills. When he encouraged the departments to meet again after the workshop, they suddenly realized that each side had been talking "*at*" rather than "*to*" the other and not hearing what was being said back. Shortly after this breakthrough, they reported to Pieroni that they had arrived at a solution that met everyone's objectives.

Effective leaders come equipped with finely tuned sonar. They can tell when it is time to move beyond skills transfer to coaching. In the past, when there was conflict on his team, says Frank Maione, former vice president of sales for Pfizer's Consumer Division, people went underground. But not after his team was aligned. Whenever he saw that there were issues, he stopped the action and reminded them that the air was getting thick; they had to get the conflict out into the open right away and resolve it. At the end of these sessions, he says, "Everyone told me that it was uncomfortable, but it was the best thing to do."

Leadership Imperative: Keep the Game and Guard the Ground Rules

Not long ago, we were working with a president of a major leisure goods designer and manufacturer who was growing increasingly concerned about slippage in performance on his top management team.

Not only were sales down for two concurrent quarters, but all the work that had been done to align the team appeared to be unraveling. The president decided to keep a performance log, which detailed the behavior of members of his team, both in full group and one-on-one meetings. It was his way of mirroring his team's behavior. On one side of the log he noted a number of the elements that constitute a high-performance team: focusing on "us" rather than "my function"; holding one another accountable; being willing to confront one another when there is disagreement; and guts—stepping up to higher performance goals. On the other side he detailed specific behavior of team members, positive and negative, against each of the entries. After a month of observation and recording, the president saw a disturbing pattern that cut across a wide swath of his team.

In the president's view, he had two options: one was to meet one on one to give feedback to team members privately. Or they could meet, full group, for a forthright and open discussion. He decided that the latter option was the way to go.

At the outset of the meeting, the president shared his performance log with the team, then asked them a number of questions: "Are my observations accurate? Do any of you have similar observations? What do you think has caused us to stray from the commitments we made during the alignment? What actions can we plan, individually and as a team, to get back on track?"

This team leader clearly understood that one of his most important tasks was to serve as keeper of the high-performance game. It is not a task for which the leader has sole responsibility, but it is up to him or her to make sure the team remains on track. By "on track," we mean that everyone is clear about and committed to the business strategy and the operational goals that flow from it; understands his or her roles and responsibilities; and adheres to the agreed-upon protocols, or ground rules, for decision making and for interpersonal behavior, especially those relating to conflict management.

Ultimately, when the leader is keeper of the game and guardian of the ground rules, he or she is looking at the team and asking: Are the members of my team playing for real—or are they just going through the motions? Is there something I am doing that should be modified or changed? What's the best way for me to hold up a mirror to members of my team to accurately reflect their behavior? How do we change?

Leadership Imperative: Raise the Bar

One of the characteristics of all great business teams is that they continually raise the performance bar. Like professional golfers who continually strive to shave a few strokes off their handicap, the best teams continually look for ways to improve. But the performance-improvement attitude is an acquired one, which often requires not-so-gentle prodding from the leader.

When Helen McCluskey joined Warnaco as president of the Intimate Apparel Group in 2004, the division was in trouble. Over the previous five years, revenue had fallen by 50% and profits were in decline. The division did not seem to have the appropriate sense of urgency, which was not very helpful, when, as McCluskey puts it, "you are fighting for your life."

McCluskey began the turnaround by stripping the team's long list of priorities down to one essential item: Intimate Apparel must reach the company's average profitability. If the company was generating 10% operating margin/profitability, the Intimate Apparel Division had to be doing the same.

McCluskey then added a heavy dose of discipline. She began holding regular monthly staff meetings, with agendas. They started on time, with or without laggards. She also role-modeled meeting behavior, showing up on time and remaining throughout the meeting. She worked with the team to establish protocols for meetings and distributed them broadly. Line-management approval processes were put in place. Specific margin targets were identified, which had to be hit during the product-development cycle to make sure profitable business was being delivered to the bottom line.

The first line-management review took place three weeks after McCluskey became president. The team got a wake-up call when she stopped the meeting dead in its tracks. Recalls McCluskey, "They weren't at any of the margin targets, so I told them that we weren't going to adopt any of the proposed styles." "But we go to market next week," the team protested. Her response: "Then we won't show anything; there is no point in selling products that will lose money. Go back and dig deeper. Work with the sourcing group, work with vendors, but get the costs down."

The team came back, one week later, with a 10-point margin improvement. McCluskey's comment was, "This is a great job. Now that you know it can be done, there is no reason for not doing it at the beginning of the process."

Unlike the team that Helen McCluskey inherited, Ken Bloom's senior team at INTTRA was already growing the business. But he insisted on raising the bar. INTTRA operates the world's leading portal for ocean containerized freight. For the first three years of its existence, says Bloom, he and his vice presidents were just trying to keep the company alive. When it became clear that the company was not just surviving, but growing at a steady rate of nearly 7% per month, the issue became: How do you transform the management team from functional experts who excel at day-to-day operations to strategic thinkers who can set and reach long-term goals?

Bloom had a clear vision of the performance he wanted to see going forward: "My goal was for every employee, all over the world, to be performing at the highest level and to be thinking strategically. We had to act before we became too big and before bad habits had a chance to set in."

The first thing Bloom did was have us interview each of his VPs to determine how strategically focused they were. The feedback showed that team members had been so immersed in urgent, day-to-day issues that they did not know how to step back and take the long view. It also revealed that members of the top team did not trust one another completely, and during the alignment session we focused on helping them improve their working relationships.

Bloom drew up a number of strategic questions for each of his VPs. For example, he asked the VP of sales: "Going forward, what will be the thrust for new business development, how will you organize around that, and what capabilities will you need?" He then brought in subject-matter consultants to work with each of the VPs to answer the questions and develop a plan to close the strategy/operations gaps. After the consultants departed, Bloom encouraged team members to role-model their newly acquired strategic acumen. He looked for ways to reinforce the high-performing behavior that the alignment session had helped instill in the VPs in order to avoid backsliding into tactical thinking and behavior. He also made sure that the level just below the VPs also went through an alignment, so the push for higher performance came from above and below. Bloom's rationale: "Once that lower level of management was prepared to operate at a higher level of performance—which included accepting more responsibility—the VPs no longer had an excuse for not letting go of the operational issues. They couldn't just pay lip service to the definition of trust that we'd agree on; they had to start walking the talk."

Bloom and his team went through the alignment session in January 2005. At the time, they were processing 18,500 containers a week. They were growing so fast that Bloom knew they would soon have to process 36,000 a week, and he was concerned that they would not have the management discipline to do it. INTTRA is now moving more than 200,000 a week with no problem and is continuing to grow, breaking records in a way its senior team never thought possible. From 2002 to 2006, the company grew 1,372%, and in 2007 it was honored as one of Deloitte's "Technology Fast 500"—a ranking of the 500 fastest-growing technology, media, telecommunications, and life sciences companies in North America.

Leadership Imperative: Be Player Centered

Leadership is, in large part, about power—about how it is exercised, shared, delegated, and used. At one extreme stand the "I lead, you follow" Alpha leaders. For them, power is positional: "I'm on top, you're on tap." For Alpha leaders at the helm, the CEO is the chief executive and the chief *enforcer*. Control is paramount to Alpha leaders; gaining subordinates' compliance is more important than winning their commitment.

At the other extreme are servant leaders. For them, power is something to be given over to subordinates rather than jealously guarded and accumulated. They are driven to lead by a desire to serve, rather than by an urge to exercise power. While Alpha leaders are not afraid to cut off a dissenting subordinate at the knees, servant leaders prefer to "wash his or her feet." Sharing, enabling, persuasion, and commitment define servant leaders.

Great leaders occupy neither extreme. In fact, it is difficult to locate high-performance leaders on any continuum of leadership power. They are not driven by the control needs of Alpha leaders; much less are they motivated by being "graciously submissive," as one advocate of servant leadership put it.

To the high-performance leader, power is a value-neutral concept. It is neither to be jealously guarded nor shared for the sake of sharing. High-performance leaders seek to *leverage* power, not monopolize it—to put it to use to drive up their team's or organization's performance. As a means to driving up results, high-performance leaders favor *"distributive power"*— putting power and authority in the hands of teams and their members, provided the conditions are right, the protocols in place, and the players sufficiently evolved to deliver maximum payoff.

All this makes becoming a player-centered leader yet another imperative of high-performance leadership. It entails judging the readiness of players to accept power and adjusting behavior accordingly, which is what the approach of Lew Frankfort, CEO and chairman of Coach, Inc., epitomizes:

> My style with each of my teams varies based on the situation and my relationship with my people. In some cases I feel very comfortable saying, 'I'm telling you to do this.' At other times, I decide to hang back, maybe to participate, but to let others take the lead. For instance, if a person is really an expert in his or her field, I don't need to do much more than provide an understanding of goals and some oversight . . . . I also coach in many ways: by modeling behavior; by consistently using rigor and logic to make decisions; by setting realistic, firm expectations; and by providing critical feedback—both constructive criticism when a person is underperforming and appreciation when they have been successful.

Astute leaders like Frankfort have an uncanny ability to focus on the capabilities of their teams. They know how to vary their decision-making behavior depending on the readiness of each team member. For example:

1. *Prescribing/directing*: telling players the what, where, when, and how of an issue
2. *Coaching/instructing*: de-emphasizing the "how" in favor of the "why"
3. *Collaborating/partnering*: working alongside the player
4. *Inspiring/empowering*: allowing team members to run with the ball[1]

How Should a Leader Behave?

Assessing player readiness requires a judgment call by the leader. The question is: On what should that judgment be based? High-performance leaders weigh two factors: the person's level of *engagement*—the degree of his or her commitment to the high-performance, horizontal model and being a team player—and the person's *skills*—the knowledge and experience he or she brings to the table.

Depending on the degree to which they are engaged and skilled, players will fall into one of four major categories. Each category requires a different approach from the leader:

1. For players with a *low* level of engagement and/or skills, the leader will need to prescribe/direct.
2. Players who possess a *moderately low* level of engagement and/or skills will benefit from coaching/instructing by the leader.
3. Players with a *moderately high* level of engagement and/or skills will respond to collaborating/partnering with the leader.
4. Players who have progressed to a *high* level of engagement and skills can be inspired/empowered by the leader.

Empowering is the most efficient leadership behavior, provided a team member has the skills and commitment to operate horizontally. In the case of the leader of a top team, empowering frees him or her from many of the day-to-day, operational concerns that divert attention from strategic issues. Empowerment at every level of management saves time by eliminating the need to go back to the leader for approval. It short-circuits conflict by removing the leader and his or her preconceived notions from the loop. It keeps accountability for decision making closest to the action. And, most importantly, it increases an organization's bench strength. It creates a new generation of leaders who will be able to take over, without trepidation, when their turn comes.

> "My toughest challenge was learning how to deal with negative feedback. At the beginning, I took it well on the outside but then overanalyzed, dwelled on it, catastrophized it. I had to learn to lighted up."
>
> — *Helen McCluskey,*
> *President, Warnaco Intimate Apparel and Swimwear Group*

The Challenge of Changing Your Leadership Behavior

The leader who has a problem adjusting his or her behavior needs to ask, "What going-in story am I holding on to that's keeping me from making this change?" and "Why?" Self-examination may be enough to break through the barrier; if not, personal coaching may be called for.

Roy Anise, vice president and general manager of Chrysalis Technologies, a division of Philip Morris USA, realized that he tended to be very directive and had trouble connecting, but when he got candid feedback from the members of his team he was surprised to learn that they judged him to be far more aggressive than he believed he was. As a result, they were uncomfortable expressing their viewpoints or making decisions on their own. He received similar feedback from his boss, which spurred him to seek coaching.

During his first session with the coach, Anise explained that, as a leader, he was unsure of how his team was progressing and where he needed to take it next. His statement prompted the coach to comment, "Now I know why you are so intimidating." "What are you talking about? I haven't said anything to you," countered Anise. "That's exactly the point," replied the coach. "You keep your cards so close to the chest, so covered up, that I have no idea what you're thinking and what's going on with you. I can see why people who work for you would feel the same sense of not knowing what's going on with you. I can see why they're intimidated."

Anise bristled at the exchange. But a day later he contacted the coach to thank him for his insight. The coach, of course, had simply been mirroring his pupil's behavior, which had caused Anise to see the light. As Anise said about his coach, "He exposed me and initially I didn't like it, but I needed to hear it." Once Anise had seen himself as others saw him, he could begin making changes. As he projected a more open, receptive image, the people on his team became more comfortable offering opinions and taking on decision-making responsibility.

Are You a Player-Centered Leader?

In many ways, changing one's leadership behavior goes against nature—or at least nurture. But, given the dynamics of the modern organization, a leader cannot afford to remain stuck in old patterns, no matter how comfortable or useful they have been in the past. The great leaders we know serve as role models for thoughtful decision making, allow players to try their decision-making wings, reward successful decisions, and reinforce learning from not-so-good ones. Then they let go.

Ask yourself the following questions to determine how well you have adapted to the player-centered leadership imperative:

1. Have you made sure that everyone on the team is committed to a common strategy and set of operational goals, clear roles and

accountabilities, protocols for decision making, and transparent business relationships?

2. Do you require that your team act as if it were a mini board of directors, in which each team member puts aside functional self-interest and owns team results?

3. To what extent have you encouraged your team members to hold one another accountable for business success? And to hold *you* accountable?

4. How attuned are you to the leader/player dynamic of each of your team members? Do you adjust your behaviors—prescribing, coaching, collaborating, inspiring—to the needs of players and circumstances?

5. Do you cling to the old leadership story, "As the leader, I get paid to make the decisions?"

6. Do team members view you as go-to gal, night watchman, referee, enabler—or as a performance-oriented facilitator/coach?

7. Do you role-model effective leadership behavior in leading your team and in how you manage upward, say, to your board of directors?

8. Think about the last time that a team member disagreed with you. Did you (a) say thank you and dispassionately assess the contrarian position; (b) use sarcasm, avoidance behavior, or seek rescuers from your team; (c) become unglued; or (d) press the eject button?

9. When was the last time you asked your team to assess your effectiveness as a leader who contributes to the team's ability to reach high-performance goals and expectations?

10. When you look at your team, do you see leaders—or followers?

Let's Follow a Leader

Believing that a picture can be worth a thousand words, we present a brief "snapshot" of one high-performing leader in action, Grant Reid, whose leadership approach illustrates many of the points we have discussed in this chapter.

As you follow Reid's actions, ask yourself how you would have handled the situation he confronted.

Before he became global president of Mars Drinks, Reid was executive vice president of sales and customer care for Mars Inc., Snack. When he assumed full responsibility for Snack sales, he faced a significant leadership challenge. Sales had not met expectations in this key strategic unit, and a quick turnaround was needed. It was akin to changing the wings on the airplane while in mid-air. We have distilled his experience into six principles that guided him during this flight.

1. Don't Bury the Past; Build on It

Reid knew that organization structure had been a big factor in the unit's failure to meet its objectives. Under the old structure, he had shared responsibility with the unit VP of sales. This had led to the usual issues related to strategy, priorities, and accountability.

One way to lead is to blame others. This was not the way Reid wanted to lead. "If the decision had been based purely on results, we would both be gone," Reid told the unit sales group in his first meeting with them. It was an honest and forthright statement, which won Reid immediate respect from his new team. Reid praised his former colleague for the way he had encouraged his associates to work with Reid to make the integrated sales group a success.

Reid stressed that, going forward, sales had to have one strategy, set of goals, and priorities that guided everyone. They were going to put the past behind them, but not before they had learned all they could from it.

2. It's All about Relationships

Leadership is as much about creating a human connection as it is about changing minds. Reid realized that his new troops would not transfer their allegiance overnight. He was going to have to work hard to win them over.

He set up individual meetings with each of the unit's vice presidents and his or her direct reports. "The first cut was not about competency, but about commitment," said Reid. "Did they believe what I was telling them? Were they comfortable with me? Would they buy into my vision?"

He encouraged them to speak openly and honestly, asking each, "How are you feeling? What are you thinking about your future here? What are your major concerns? How can I help?"

As they responded, he used active listening skills to identify the underlying messages. He was particularly attuned to body language. "If someone tells you they're really committed while they're looking at their shoes, be concerned," he advises.

Reid learned that people wanted reassurance that their future was secure. He explained to people what their roles would be, what they should focus on, and what was going to change. He also promised that he was not going to play favorites.

3. Don't Just Lead Your Team—Be a Part of It

Throughout his career, Grant Reid has gone beyond "management by *walking* around" to "management by *working* around." Early in his career, as plant manager at an M&Ms plant, Reid made a point of actually doing every job in the plant. He connected hoses, put sugar into the storage hoppers, melted cocoa butter, ran the packaging equipment—even swept the floor. All because he believes deeply that a leader must understand the business and the people that make it run. "After that, when we had a meeting and people talked about a problem with a particular piece of obscure equipment, I knew exactly what they were talking about. I had helped to run that machine."

Remember Chuck Nesbit's point about the lieutenant in Iraq who needs to drive the Humvee? Reid also believes that leaders should not ask others to do things they would not do themselves. "Once, when we had a major storm, we didn't close the plant for the night shift. I made sure that I was there with my associates." It bought Reid a lot of equity, but that is not why he did it. "It's not enough for a leader to say, 'We're all in this together.' You have to show, by your actions, that you are part of the team—not above it."

4. Help Everyone Become a High Performer

Grant Reid made good on his promise to forge a new, unified sales team where everyone's contribution would be valued equally. Over 600 people from the central sales organization were integrated into Snack's sales group, and the process went smoothly because Reid and his team saw to it that they received the skills they needed to work together as a seamless, high-performing team.

Reid began by getting agreement from his vice presidents on Snack's future strategy. The newly integrated team revisited the strategy that was already in place, reconfirming that it was the right one and that the five key strategic initiatives that stemmed from it were still the team's highest priorities.

After ensuring that his VPs were aligned around strategy and goals, Reid quickly moved to align them around the other elements that make for a high-performing team: roles and responsibilities; protocols, or rules of engagement for making decisions and dealing with conflict; and business relationships, or mutual expectations of how they would behave vis-à-vis one another. Everyone was encouraged to hold one another—and Reid—responsible for achieving Snack results.

Reid did not stop here. He continued to cascade the alignment process down through Snack, aligning teams below the vice-president level so they too could achieve the highest possible level of performance.

5. Show How It's Done

On great teams, candor is king. Reid set the tone when he engaged in "straight talk" about Snack's failure to meet its sales goals, the replacement of the unit VP, and the need for radical change. He encouraged the old and new members of his team to respond in kind. He told them that he wanted them to challenge him. "If I ask the seven people on my team if they agree with me, and all seven say 'yes,' I might as well get rid of six of them," Reid told his VPs. "I want to hear the contrarian view."

He went further. In front of his team, he is comfortable challenging his boss when he feels things are moving too slowly—role-modeling the upward confrontation that he expects from the players on his team.

6. Park Your Ego

Leadership is not about "me," but "us"—and getting results. Steely, quiet confidence trumps brassy displays of infallibility. Effective leaders in a high-performance environment possess a special kind of self-confidence—the ability to admit to not having all the answers.

"Putting your ego aside and asking others to help find answers isn't something everyone can do," says Reid. "It takes a very strong person to relinquish control in the interest of finding the best solution." Such solutions come when leaders harness collective brainpower.

HOW GREAT LEADERS SEE THEMSELVES

We asked a number of great leaders with whom we have worked to tell us what they see as their major role on their team. If you have not been part of a high-performing team, you may find some of their answers surprising:

"My job is to keep people on track and make sure they take full accountability and responsibility for their own work and their peers'. I also have to make sure that I carry out my commitments regarding the things I am responsible for."
      —*Joe Pieroni, President and CEO, Daiichi Sankyo Inc.*

"I view myself as a mentor and teacher more than as a director of people. I serve as a sounding board. I give perspective. I ask questions. I provide people with the resources they need and allow them to be in situations where they can succeed. I also give them the latitude to make mistakes and learn from them— even if it means stopping myself from intervening while they do it."
      —*Chuck Nesbit, EVP and COO, Chico's FAS, Inc.*

"My role is to keep our global organization all moving in the same direction, touch as many people as possible to mobilize the organization broadly, and recruit key talents. Also, to coach direct reports one-on-one when they are feeling pressure."
      —*David Epstein, President and CEO, Novartis Oncology*

"My role as a leader is to be more collaborative, to help in goal setting—getting everyone on the same path, setting the broader vision and very specific goals. My HR team wanted a stronger voice at the executive table; they wanted me to put the 'people agenda' out front and center, and that's what I have done."
      —*David Greenberg, SVP HR, L'Oréal USA*

> "As an organization, we are making good progress toward my becoming the questioner, the coach, and not a content expert. I personally add much more value by asking the questions, making sure the right people are working on the issues, and spending my time thinking about strategic issues."
> —*Frank Verwiel, CEO, Axcan Pharma*
>
> "My job is having the right people in place. If I do that successfully, we will have a well-balanced group that has the complementary skills to solve any problem as a team. I have to provide the right environment and opportunities. Sometimes it requires asking questions, sometimes it requires coaching. It depends on the situation and the people involved."
> —*Helen McCluskey, President, Warnaco Intimate Apparel and Swimwear Group*

End Thought

To understand leaders, you must understand their followers. So goes much of the standard patter on the subject. No doubt the insight is a valid one, especially within the context of hierarchical organizations, where there is a clear-cut delineation between leaders and followers. But, as organizations evolve horizontally, the traditional leader–follower paradigm is no longer a fruitful construct. On great business teams, "followers" assume many of the same behaviors and traits previously ascribed only to leaders.

What are these behaviors and traits? What personal transformation must a player undergo to move from good to great? In our next chapter, we will shift the focus from the leader to the team as we answer these and other questions about The New High-Performance Player.

Note

1. For an in-depth discussion of each of the leadership behaviors and when to use them, see Appendix A.

3

The New High-Performance Player

The Price of Admission

When one executive we know became CEO of a global telecom company, he looked around at his top players and was struck by what he had discovered—there was no top management team. What he had was a loose confederation of executives who were highly motivated and functionally adept, but they shared no common sense of mission or goals and had no concept of working interdependently to solve problems and make decisions.

The new CEO was told that there had been limited communication between the team and his predecessor, who had never involved his senior executives in setting strategy. What the "team" lacked in long-term strategy it made up for with ad hoc projects, which cumulatively created a kind of direction by default. Competitive threats were dealt with on the fly, and often at the eleventh hour. Results were achieved by trial and error, with little sustainability.

There were no formal management team meetings. Instead, the top executives huddled when an issue arose, and only in subgroups. Potentially contentious issues were either not brought up—"I don't see any dead elephant's head on the conference table, do you?"—or were dealt with off line by triangulating, going underground, or enlisting supporters around the water cooler.

And there was limited accountability. When a complex and multifunctional issue arose no one would take ownership. "No one wanted to catch it," says the CEO, "so it was tossed around like a hot potato."

The team that this executive inherited was obviously not a great one. Chances are, if it had been faced with the kind of challenges that confronted Applied Biosystems, Chico's, Novartis Oncology, or Mars Inc. Latin America, it would not have been able to rise to the occasion. It had no clear sense of strategy, no willingness to handle contentious issues, and no sense of "us." It would not make it to the Q School, much less qualify for pro competition.

This top team was not alone. Similarly underperforming entities can be found in nearly all organizations, at every level. In fact, in a national study we did for the American Society for Quality,[1] 1,905 managers and individual contributors, in a cross-section of industries, told us that less than half of their organizations' project teams always/often meet their goals and only one-third are always/often completed on time and on budget.

But even seriously underperforming teams can rebound to greatness. In the previously mentioned telecom company, for example, the change has been significant. The transformation started when the entire top team met—in itself a first—to set a gutsy new strategy that has provided a consistent framework for day-to-day decision making. New-technology developments and strategic alliances, once an afterthought of the top team, have become a business imperative, leading to unprecedented top- and bottom-line growth in the past two years. The top team now meets on a regular basis to raise and resolve critical business issues, including those that were once too hot to handle. There is a new commitment to winning not for individuals or their function, but for the team and the company.

How does a team like this get there? Not by restructuring, group bonding, or mega-organization-change initiatives. The road to a great team begins at the two nuclear elements of team reality—the leader and team members. Efforts are targeted directly toward first changing the "inner" performance game—how the team leader and members perceive themselves and their team—and then reframing or realigning the patterns of team interaction. For team members, the inner change is just as profound as that of the leader, which we described in the previous chapter. It begins with the question: *What are the characteristics and behaviors that constitute the "price of admission" for membership on a high-performing team?*

Consider the following lists of characteristics, which were developed by two teams within the same organization—one the senior team, the other its direct reports—as they started out on the road to high performance. They asked themselves, "If this were a great business team, how would a team member show up?"

From the Novartis OTC Global Leadership Team:
- Be personally accountable and hold others accountable.
- Be coachable: adapt, move, change, and lead others to change.
- Be collaborative: open, above board, direct.
- Be trusting: let go so others can lead.
- Have integrity: keep your word.
- Be committed: act as an owner, really engage/add value.
- Etc.

From a Novartis OTC Global Category Team:
- Follow up/act upon decisions.
- Keep commitments.
- Follow conflict-resolution protocols.
- Be good listeners.
- Be open/transparent.
- Act as coaches/support each other.
- Etc.

These traits are clearly what you would expect from teams headed in a high-performance, horizontal direction—being open/transparent, acting as an owner of the team's results, extending accountability, adhering to protocols for managing conflict, and the like. Just as the leader of a great business team must undergo a personal transformation in order to meet the challenges of this new model, each member of the team must undergo a similar transformation. The list of characteristics must move off the easel sheets and into how each team member shows up and behaves.

The Mindset of a Great Player

It takes a private revolution to become a fully evolved, high-performance player. It begins with a mind-set change. The leader, as we have seen, is responsible for the *collective* mindset of the team, providing a safe environment in which candor and accountability are possible, without fear of repercussions from anyone—including the leader. In this sense, the leader facilitates the personal transformation of the players, but it is up to them to do the heavy lifting required to change their way of thinking in four ways.

1. Think Like a Director

Manuel Jessup, chief HR officer for Chico's FAS, Inc., likens the mind-set of great team members to that of the individuals on an athletic team—when the team wins, everyone wins; when it loses, everyone shares in the loss. It is a good analogy. Another, from business rather than sports, is equally apt: The members of great teams think like members of a board of directors. They keep their eye on the overarching goal, the results the company needs to achieve to stay on top of the competition. They are interested in the health of the company as a whole, not in any one area or function. And, knowing that time is money, they put a premium on swift, effective action. They are committed to maximizing ROI with every decision.

Chuck Nesbit, executive vice president and COO of Chico's, points out the changes that have occurred as his colleagues have made this shift in mindset, "Issues get handled in the moment and don't get tabled. People are not willing to sit there and let issues go unresolved. If progress is being impeded, if two leaders are letting something fester, a team member will address the issue."

Chico's has cascaded the high-performing team model to the second tier of management, and Nesbit believes that the changes in this group's way of thinking have been dramatic. "In the past," he comments, "they might have waited for direction. Now, they have stepped up to the plate and begun taking action. They tell the top team what they have decided after the fact, not before. For example, the head of planning and allocation came in and said, 'Based on what I see happening in the business, I think we are going to have an inventory imbalance in six weeks. I think we need to run a special sale next week.'"

2. Put Team First, Function Second

Company directors are focused on overall business results rather than being emotionally invested in any single business unit or function. So too are members of high-performing teams. They have learned to rebalance their attachment to the specific function they represent. They are team members first and functional representatives second. They do not show up looking for the biggest handout at feeding time (i.e., the annual budget cycle) unless a solid business case can be made for doing so. They contribute their technical expertise across functions when it is needed. And they do not hesitate to weigh in on the performance of other functions when they sense problems.

At Chico's, CEO Scott Edmonds and his direct reports were the first to move to the high-performing team model. Nesbit says that they have "really elevated their game. They are overseeing their functions, but they are aware of the interdependencies and are taking ownership for moving the total game along. In the past, a marketing person might have said, 'I got out the catalog and the announcements that we are having a sale. If somebody doesn't get the merchandise from the distribution center to the store in time, that's not my fault. That's someone else's job.' Now, we're more likely to hear Marketing say, 'The catalog is due to arrive in customers' homes on February 15. I want to make sure we maximize the effect of the advertising. I want to make sure that the sale is a success. How are we going to make sure we get those goods in place?'"

Nesbit has seen this new mindset throughout the company, as more managers are getting out into the stores, listening to the customers, and bringing back feedback and their interpretations of what they have learned. He hears statements such as, "We didn't buy enough inventory to take advantage of this opportunity. It's clear that we could sell more. Here's what I suggest we do." In the past, he recalls, they were much more likely to say, "Somebody else is responsible for buying; my job is to get what they buy to the stores. I did my job. They didn't. Too bad."

Not everyone at Chico's found it easy to rewire his or her thinking. "There were a couple of people who were still more concerned about individual contributions and how they could pole-vault their personal career, as opposed to thinking about the total team," says Jessup. He gave these individuals feedback on their attitude, and they were receptive. They have asked him to continue calling them on their behavior when he senses that they are slipping back into old thinking patterns, and he plans to continue doing so.

On a great business team, siloed thinking is out, but in the course of doing business it is hard to get away from it. The limits of functional roles and responsibilities are not always clear; departments share services and space; they compete for finite resources; their managers compete for promotions; and so on. A certain amount of conflict is bound to arise, even on a great team. When it does, it is dealt with quickly and directly.

Mark Stevenson, executive vice president of Applied Biosystems, was a member of the senior team that Cathy Burzik shepherded to high performance. He recalls that, "At the start, we had to deal with conflicts between functions that had a lot of overlap. The team insisted that the involved parties identify the issues that existed between them and then work together to get resolution. This continued during the first six months, as we learned to get rid of silos and operate like a board of directors."

3. Embrace Accountability

At the end of the 2006 fiscal year, a sizable financial shortfall in one of its business units caught the senior management team of a food services company off guard. On further investigation, the CEO learned that the head of the unit had been aware of the problems for several months but had not taken any action. Two of his team members had also known what was going on, but they remained silent as the situation spiraled out of control. This was a classic case of the "it's not my job" syndrome.

These executives had not climbed very high up the rungs of the Accountability Ladder illustrated in Figure 3.1. To do so would require them to undergo a significant mindset change around the question: What am I accountable for?

What would be your answer to this question? If you said, "me and my department," then you are stuck, like the food service executives, on the bottom two rungs of the ladder, which is typical in a hierarchical environment. Think how different their behavior—and the outcome—would have been if these executives had reoriented their thinking and assumed accountability not only for their own performance, but also for that of their peers, their leader, and ultimately, their organization.

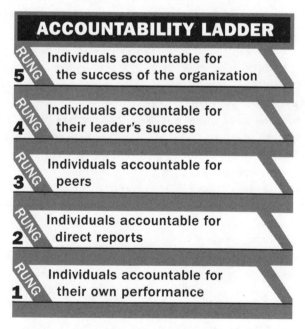

Figure 3.1 The Accountability Ladder

Holding Peers Accountable

The first and second rungs of the Accountability Ladder pose next to no challenge. It is the way things are. The third rung is where things get interesting and high performance kicks in.

At this point, the leader is no longer the rescuer to whom team members outsource their intelligence and judgment. Instead, team members tackle problems head-on and find their own solutions, without retreating to "higher-ups." Those problems run the gamut from cut-and-dried business issues to those touchy ones involving one another's performance.

If you were a fly on the wall listening to a conversation between two high-performance team members, here is what you might hear:

> "Hey, Jason, the new product launch plan developed by Marketing covers all the bases, but I haven't seen a sales plan from you, especially one dealing with key accounts."
>
> "I'm not really that concerned, Peter. We've brought on additional reps and the new commission plan you guys in Finance helped us put in place provides all the motivation we need."
>
> "Great, Jason, but the last time we went to market with a new offering it fell flat because of poor sales planning. We didn't target the key accounts, didn't have a good lead-tracking system in place, and many of the reps had paper-thin product knowledge. The poor results affected all of us, even us bean counters in Finance."
>
> "Peter, I can assure you that history won't repeat itself."
>
> "I'm sure you're right, Jason, but why don't we schedule a team meeting to review your plan and provide input?"
>
> "Sounds like a good idea. Let me think about it."
>
> "Okay Jason, but let me get back to you by the end of the week to talk over the next steps."

What you would be listening to is straight talk, plain and simple. On the surface, it sounds so logical and straightforward—one executive critically questioning a peer and pressing for an action to advance the common good. Why, then, is such talk not more typical? Because it takes a mindset breakthrough to make it happen. And without having the elements of great business teams in place, the breakthrough required to move up to Rung 3 and beyond is unlikely to occur.

How do you get team members to break through the barriers that prevent them from calling one another on behaviors that compromise the achievement of business results? The leader plays a central role in convincing players that they are not only permitted but *expected* to start holding one another accountable.

Stephanie Black Allen, organization development consultant to Wyeth's Consumer Healthcare Division, recalls that when she began working with a new innovation team, "holding up a mirror to the group was important until they were able to do it themselves." When the team was first created, says Allen, team members looked to the leader of their department or organizational area for guidance in dealing with one another. They had to be weaned away from decision dependency. Now, she says, "People are more willing to address issues one on one, as members of the same team rather than functional reps. On a day-to-day basis, they hold each other accountable, saying, 'This is what we agreed and how we said we would interact with each other. You haven't kept up your end of the bargain. What are we going to do about it?'"

One of the biggest barriers to peer-to-peer and player-to-leader accountability involves depersonalizing feedback. This was a real problem for Roy Anise, vice president and general manager of Chrysalis Technologies, a division of Philip Morris USA, and his team. Anise says that "Their self-worth always seemed to be on trial. They didn't understand that being questioned didn't imply being criticized personally." Anise helped the team break out of this mindset by role-modeling willingness to take accountability for his performance and depersonalizing feedback. He told them that if they saw him not living up to his commitments and came to him with that feedback, he would view it as a gift. He even distributed a number of Starbucks gift cards to his team and asked them to give one back to him each time he transgressed, so they would feel as though they were giving him a gift.

Ken Bloom, CEO of INTTRA, is a leader who has devoted considerable think-time to overcoming barriers to accountability. His advice: Be sure to manage consequences carefully. As he put its, "There has to be some degree of immunity for this model to work. It's up to the leader to make sure that there's no punishment for the lapse for which a peer is holding another accountable." Otherwise, you run up against the situation that Mao Zedong faced with his so-called Hundred Flowers Campaign. He encouraged everyone to openly express themselves, only to imprison or shoot those who voiced opposition.

Bloom has seen several other factors get in the way of peers holding peers accountable, including the fact that, "It's easier to get candor than receptivity. People are fairly open to saying what they think, but when others tell *them* the truth it is more difficult for them to accept. Getting people to not be defensive was the hardest part." He has also had problems with people who were "too nice" and didn't want to hurt others' feelings by calling them on the carpet. "Niceness is fine," says Bloom, "but it's not a performance virtue. Helping a colleague step up his or her level of play is." Also, he adds, "If people have been high-performing contributors in the past, when their performance starts to slip there's a tendency to give them a little slack. You have to impress upon the team that it's the organization

MAKING ACCOUNTABILITY WORK

How do you go about getting peers to hold peers accountable? Short of going through wholesale team realignment, here are two quick actions that work well. First, have your team list the key behaviors that, in their estimation, constitute best practices in teamwork. Some of these relate to mindset, some to skills, and some to the protocols that the team has agreed to live by. To illustrate:

- Be open and candid; say what is on your mind.
- Play for the team, not yourself or your function.
- Act like an "owner": Be engaged, add value, keep the team on track.
- Be personally accountable: Deliver on promises, meet deadlines
- Hold one another accountable for delivering business results.
- Hold one another accountable for resolving interpersonal conflicts.
- Be receptive to feedback *from others:* Listen carefully, depersonalize, and change your behavior accordingly.

- Base feedback *to others* on observable behavior; deliver feedback objectively, without personalizing or blaming.
- Act as a coach to team members in need.
- Observe the protocols, or ground rules, by which the team has agreed to operate.

Next, have each member of the team rate every other member—including the team leader—on how his or her behavior stacks up against the list. To capture the ratings, we recommend using a five-point Lichert scale, with 1 signifying "Never" and 5 signifying "Always." Then, each person has an opportunity to see how the others have rated him or her: perceived strengths, areas of concerns, areas that require behavior change.

The first time your team members assess one another, the aim is to develop a baseline, or snapshot, of current behavior, how it needs to change, and a plan for doing so. Then, it is time to go live. Tie the assessment—which we recommend conducting twice a year—to the performance appraisal and rewards process.

Warning: Without an impartial, skilled facilitator, this exercise could be injurious to your team's health and performance.

that matters, not the individual. Everyone has to be held as accountable today as they were two years ago."

Holding the Leader Accountable

For those who have been trained in the "leader is always right" school of management, moving to the fourth rung of the Accountability Ladder requires a giant leap. Here, a player does not hesitate to deliver this message to the leader: "I share accountability for this team's results. If you don't get the business results you've promised, if you don't observe our agreed-upon rules, or if you violate the team's behavior code, I will be obligated to call you on it." It is not for team members with weak stomachs or leaders with fragile egos.

Recall the conversations that Novartis's Larry Allgaier initiates when he senses that members of his team are reluctant to give him negative feedback on his performance. Allgaier gives them his tacit permission, in a very subtle way. Joe Amado, vice president of information services and CIO of Philip Morris USA, has actually formalized the process by which his team holds him accountable. Every year, he asks the members of his IT team to complete a "leadership scorecard" on him. "It's like 360-degree feedback," Amado explains, "but it's not on paper. It's person to person." Joe kicks off a half-day meeting, then leaves his team members to confer among themselves to answer questions in four major categories: How well does Amado allocate resources? Provide direction? Build capabilities? Give feedback on performance?

When he comes back into the room, they give him their honest feedback. Amado carefully considers their input and then makes any adjustments needed to further his personal journey to high performance.

Feedback on great business teams is not typically a brutal, punishing experience for the leader who receives it or the players who give it. David Epstein actually likes it when team members hold him accountable, as long as their feedback is well grounded and logical. In his view, "The people who speak up and stir the pot help me make the right decisions. They help me make sure the organization is moving in the right direction; if they point out that we are off course, I'm always willing to make changes."

Nor does holding the leader accountable necessarily mean taking him or her to task for underperformance. It may simply entail raising an issue that has not been brought up before or resurfacing an issue that has fallen off the radar screen so a solution can be hammered out.

For example, when Cathy Burzik led the senior team at Applied Biosystems, she certainly was not shirking her duty or underperforming, but in the view of her team she needed to refocus her attention. As Mark Stevenson describes it, "Cathy had a tendency to want to get involved in the details. We pointed out to her that we felt she should be focusing on the 'go forward strategy' for the company. She listened and was agreeable to our taking over more and more of the operational details. She became comfortable enough to take off a full week to celebrate her wedding anniversary. We told her, 'Go and enjoy yourself; we can operate the business without you,' and she did just that."

While confronting a leader may be uncomfortable at first, there are strategies that will enhance your chances of being listened to—if not enthusiastically, at least respectfully—and of having a real impact on those decisions that fall within the leader's zone of accountability.

Later in this chapter, we will go into more detail about the full range of skills that high-performance team members need to acquire, but for now we will mention two that are critical in player–leader interactions: delivering feedback and influencing others.

Delivering feedback is a skill about which many books and articles have been written. Here, we will just reiterate four cardinal rules that it is always wise to follow—and never more so than when entering into a conversation with the person you report to.

1. *Pay attention to time and place.* While there are times when it may be appropriate to question the leader's behavior in front of others, it is almost always better to deliver your message in a private, one-on-one meeting. If you have any doubts at all, arrange a talk behind closed doors, at a time when you will not be interrupted.
2. *Focus on the facts.* There is never any room for emotion or personal attacks when delivering feedback, whether to another team member or to the leader. Stick to commenting on the specific behavior you have observed—or failed to observe—and the tangible consequences for the team.
3. *Take full responsibility.* You are not there to represent others, unless you have been asked to serve as spokesperson for the team. State clearly that you are only voicing *your* opinion and relating *your* observations. Do not put words into other people's mouths.
4. *Contextualize the discussion.* Look for ways to frame the discussion within the larger context of the organization's strategy, operational plan, or team charter, and then point to the impact of a leader's behavior on these. Back in Chapter 2, this is precisely what Scott Edmond's team did when they called him on paying too much attention to a nonstrategic acquisition.

When it comes to influencing others to your point of view, the best way we know to do this is to present a clear, compelling business case. Do your homework. Come armed with facts and figures. Do not just say, "Unless you change X and Y, we're headed for disaster." Monetize the discussion: "Our overtime costs shot up 200% last month because of the hiring freeze in Production" or "We lost $750,000 in sales because the product launch was delayed by five weeks."

4. Become Comfortable with Discomfort

On a great business team, expectations are high. As we have seen, peers hold peers and their leader accountable for the behaviors and commitments to which the team has agreed. Breakdowns are surfaced and resolved quickly and in a nonjudgmental way, creating a clean and level playing field that allows the team to move swiftly toward its goals. But because this is not natural or typical organizational behavior, learning to do so often constitutes a "rite of passage" for team members.

Each team member must learn to move out of his or her personal comfort zone and become comfortable with discomfort. Some people find the transition liberating—even exhilarating; others are never able to overcome their reticence. Most get there eventually, but it can be a long, difficult journey.

This is another area in which the leader can facilitate mindset change by paying careful attention to players' needs, individually and as a group. Ken Bloom advises leaders that, "When people are having problems with these new ideas, you have to tell them, 'You may not like taking this role, but you have to. It's your job.'"

Roy Anise is another leader who takes a tough-love approach to candor and accountability. Many members of his team came from an area of the company where the prevailing mode was command and control. As a result, when they were first asked to give one another feedback, they were very uneasy with the process. Anise realized that they were going to need a lot more practice in this area. "I don't think you can overinvest in facilitating conversations in which people receive honest feedback and internalize it. They have to be uncomfortable going through the experience, or they are not really hearing the straight story."

Anise was disappointed when, even after an alignment, players were still reluctant to give one another, and him, feedback. He told them, "We all have a responsibility to identify any performance issue that we feel is impacting how we perform. We made an agreement to do that, and even if it is uncomfortable we must honor that agreement."

The Skill Set of a Great Player

Changing a player's mindset is only half the high-performance equation. Providing the skill set that can take a player from good to great is equally important.

The Player as Leader/Influencer

At its simplest level, leadership is the art of getting others to do your bidding or, more formally, it is a process of *influencing* the activities of an individual or group in efforts of goal achievement.

Sure, those who are charismatic, brilliant, superb communicators, and crackerjack strategic thinkers tend to rise to leadership positions. But leadership is a practical art, and, genetic endowment aside, much of it can be learned. On a great business team, every member is expected to master the basic leadership skills needed to influence his or her teammates to achieve the highest level of performance.

If a case needs to be made for the need to acquire the "soft" leadership skills to play effectively on a great business team, we think Manuel Jessup, chief human resources officer at Chico's, states it persuasively: "Once you have created a high-performance culture, you need to give people the skills to enable them to thrive in that culture. You have to have the right players, with innate ability. But regardless of how smart you are intellectually, if you don't have the 'soft' skills such as active listening, assertion, and conflict management, it won't work. For example, people who want to have a candid conversation, but don't possess conflict resolution skills, can't do it effectively."

On any team, players require three types of skills: technical, strategic, and leadership. The need for the first two will vary according to an individual's position in the organization. Technical skills are most important at the first level of management and below, and strategic skills increase in importance as individuals rise through the ranks of management. But, as a member of a team of leaders, every player on every great team needs the same degree of proficiency in leadership skills, including the ability to influence others.

It is a lesson that David Waldock, senior vice president of sales for L'Oréal Paris, learned as he moved his team along the horizontal playing field. "When we began moving toward the high-performance model," says Waldock, "we assumed too much. We thought people would get it and start using the leadership skills after a couple of formal sessions. What we didn't account for was that many members of our top team in Sales had been promoted because they had excellent technical and executional skills, but they were quite junior in the sense that they had less practice in leadership positions. After the alignment, we gave them as much additional exposure to and practice with the skills as time permitted."

Was the effort worth it? "It was invaluable," concludes Waldock. "I'm not sure we would be functioning well today if we hadn't made the commitment we did. We have expanded our sales activities and brand initiatives. And we've done it without increasing headcount. Instead, we have learned to be much more efficient and much clearer in our communication. We get to conclusions much faster. We are no longer a team just on paper, working independently. We have a real group dynamic now, and it's a good one."

The exercise of power does not necessarily require social savvy, whereas the ability to influence others clearly does. To be an effective influencer requires a keen ability both to *assess where others stand* vis-à-vis you and your agenda and to *be aware of how you behave with others.*

Assessing Where Others Stand

Look around you, both at members of your team and at others in your organization with whom you interact. How likely is each of these people to be an ally, a foe, or something in between?

As you think about the question, consider two variables—the degree to which they agree with you and the amount of support they are willing to provide you. In our experience with this exercise, we find that people tend to fall into five basic categories. Following is a short description of each type of individual, along with some tips for influencing them:[2]

1. *Double Dealers* agree with you at the business-concept level but have for some reason decided to withhold their support. Focus on listening to their concerns, encouraging them to speak candidly, and working to build trust between you.
2. *Foes* neither agree with your goals, nor are they among your supporters. Influencing foes can be a Herculean task. Encourage candor, "story" sharing, and the forging of new agreements for moving ahead.
3. *Members of the Loyal Opposition* support you while disagreeing with your point of view. They trust you but are at odds with your approach to an issue. Present a strong business case, as objectively as possible, to turn your colleagues around.
4 and 5. *Partners* and *Middle-of-the-Roaders* present opportunities. The former group supports you and agrees with you. Having them in

your corner is an excellent way to demonstrate to others the value of your ideas. The Partners can have a positive influence on others, especially the Middle-of-the-Roaders.

These thumbnail sketches are obvious simplifications, but the point of the exercise is to begin to develop the social antennae and influencing skills required to be an effective leader or player on a great business team.

Being Aware of How You Behave

The second key to influencing others is to be acutely aware of *your own* interpersonal behavior. First, how do you typically go about seeking to exert influence over others? No one's behavior pattern is the same in every situation or with every person he or she meets. However, most of us usually operate within a limited area of the Behavioral Continuum, shown in Figure 3.2. Docile lambs rarely, if ever, turn into raging bulls, or vice versa.

We often ask teams to go through a simple exercise as a first step toward becoming aligned in the area of business relationships. Each player tells the group where his or her behavior falls on the continuum, and then the rest of the team weighs in. You would be amazed at how often we see a huge disconnect between how a player views him- or herself and colleagues' perceptions. This is particularly true of people who are viewed as quite aggressive by others, yet see themselves as, at most, highly assertive. It is a real eye-opener.

Behavior in dealing with conflict is especially revealing. So, we also ask players to think about how they generally handle potentially contentious situations. We ask them to think about two dimensions—assertiveness and cooperativeness. *Assertiveness* is the extent to which a person attempts to satisfy his or her own needs. *Cooperativeness* is the extent to which an individual attempts to satisfy another person's needs.

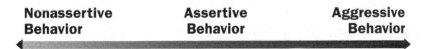

Figure 3.2 The Behavioral Continuum

Depending on the degree of balance they possess between these two elements, people tend to adopt one of five distinct methods of dealing with conflict.[3]

1. *Compete*: be assertive and uncooperative, more interested in pursuing his or her own concerns at the expense of others.
2. *Accommodate*: be unassertive and cooperative, choosing to neglect his or her own concerns in order to satisfy the concerns of others.
3. *Avoid*: be unassertive and uncooperative, choosing not to take any action and allowing conflict to remain unresolved.
4. *Compromise*: be squarely in the middle in terms of both assertiveness and cooperativeness, resulting in a solution that may be mutually acceptable yet only partially satisfying to each side.
5. *Collaborate*: be both assertive and cooperative, willing to work together to find a solution that fully satisfies the concerns of each.

While players are thinking about how they prefer to deal with conflict, it is a good idea for them to also do some analysis of their peers' and leader's typical modus operandi in this area.

Armed with this increased knowledge about themselves and their peers, team members have a much better understanding of how much of a challenge it is going to be to successfully influence others to their points of view. And, after taking a hard, honest look in the mirror, they also see how their own behavior may be keeping them from developing the trust and respect that they need in order to become influential leaders in the new environment.

Being a Skilled Relationship Builder

Great team members recognize that it is not enough for everyone on a team to agree on strategy, goals, roles, and protocols. Building solid business relationships is equally important. Stephanie Black Allen, referring to business relationships—the fifth area in which teams need to be aligned—uses the analogy of a family going on vacation: "Yes, you have to know where you are going and what you want it to look like when you get there, but the question is, When you put everybody in the car together, how is the trip going to unfold? How do people take the journey together?"

When we align a team around business relationships, we introduce them to the skills that they are going to need in order to address the interpersonal issues that are bound to surface during the journey. And there are always lots of them. Just like the vacationing family that cannot agree on the best route, when to stop for lunch, or which motel to pull into, team members will always have opinions and needs that will be at variance. And, while parents generally settle family differences, on great business teams it is unacceptable for the leader to serve *in loco parenti;* players are expected to resolve their own differences.

Whenever two people have needs that appear to be incompatible, the potential for conflict between them exists. As a player, the skills you need will vary according to the circumstances. For example:

- When *another player's needs* are pressing you need *active listening skills:* the ability to clarify, understand, and acknowledge another's point of view.
- When *your needs* are pressing you need *assertion skills*: the ability to state your case from a position of strength, rather than being passive or running over others. In other words, occupying the assertive rather than the nonassertive or aggressive section of the Behavioral Continuum.
- When *both players' needs* are pressing you need *conflict-management skills:* the ability to manage each party's perceptions to defuse emotions, create a common understanding of the real issues at hand, and work toward a collaborative solution in which everyone "wins."

Regarding conflict-management skills, John Doumani, now managing director, Fonterra, Australia–New Zealand, sums up his experience providing such skills when he was president, international for Campbell Soup:

Looking at conflict situations as part of the job, as a business case, doesn't come easily, but it's critical that people learn how to do it. They also need to become aware of the impact they have on others and to learn how to process the feedback they get from their colleagues. They don't learn these lessons unless you are willing to put a lot of time and energy into modeling the behavior and building the skill base in the organization. We put in place quite a few conflict-resolution and influence training modules—not just for the leadership team, but throughout the organization—as a way to get people moving in the right direction. At first, it was hard for people to change their behavior, but as people practiced the skills they became second nature. The way our organization viewed conflict, and dealt with it, really changed.

What listening, assertion, and conflict-management skill sets entail and how players go about becoming proficient in them is discussed at length in Appendix B, and in the following chapter we will provide a number of examples of how players grapple with using them in real-life situations.

What Causes Players to Derail?

In management Shangri-la, great players on great teams remain at the top of their game. In the real world, greatness is fragile and derailment can occur, even when the leader provides an environment of candor and accountability, aligns the team, invests in skill development, and role-models the expected behaviors. Some team members will still have trouble. Here are some of the most frequent barriers they encounter, along with advice from great leaders on how to overcome them.

- *The inability to change going-in stories and core limiting beliefs*

Call it a finger-on-the-hot-stove moment: A past event, especially a high-impact one, occurs and then gets forever locked into our memory bank. "The last time I opened my mouth in a meeting, it cost me a raise." The next time around, grinning and bearing it will likely become the meeting behavior of choice. How we react to a given situation depends in large part on our past experience in the same or similar situations. Past experience creates present expectations.

Over time, such expectations can become core limiting beliefs. These act as self-censors that unconsciously constrict behavior. "I'm just not comfortable enough to express myself well publicly. For me, silence is golden." In other words, core limiting beliefs give rise to "stories" that we tell ourselves when we confront situations. They exercise, often unconsciously, great pull on behavior.

Getting individual team members to let go of stories and core limiting beliefs is often one of the most difficult tasks the leader, other players, and individual coaches can undertake. Most of us are simply unaware of the stories and beliefs that hold us back. And we are often extremely uncomfortable talking about situations in which we feel threatened or inadequate.

Brian Camastral, regional president, Latin America for Mars Inc., remembers how difficult it was for him to get one team member to open up and share her story. One of the corporate staff officers whom Camastral had asked to join the senior team had the necessary skills and ability, but what struck Camastral early on was the executive's lack of commitment, which began slowing down the team. It took three one-on-one dinners between her and Camastral before she felt comfortable enough to let her real feelings come out. She disclosed to Camastral that she was terrified that the Latin American operation was undergoing a huge transformation: from a local, fairly autonomous operation to a high-performing, interdependent organization where speed, accountability, and communication were paramount. Her story was that her lack of a college degree would prevent her from functioning in the sophisticated new environment. Camastral reassured her that he did not care about how much education she had; he was only concerned with how effectively she did her job, and he gave her high marks for her performance. "She accepted my reassurance," relates Camastral, "and within two weeks there was a night-to-day transformation in her. She delivered the highest quantity and some of the best quality work and became the most influential person on the team."

Looking back on this hurdle and others he had to overcome while getting his new team to embrace the high-performance model, Camastral notes that he did not begin to crack the toughest issues on the team until he began engaging team members one on one, probing into their background and experience, learning what made them tick and making them sufficiently comfortable to disclose what they would rather not have revealed about the stories that were blocking their performance.

■ *Turning a deaf ear to feedback*

The ear is a wonderful instrument for facilitating learning, self-development, and personal change—provided the messages get through and are then processed. This is often not the case, especially when the messages carry negative feedback. That is when we tend to turn a deaf ear.

Another member of Brian Camastral's team either did not hear or chose not to hear Camastral's feedback. The executive was quick to offer opinions but slow to assume accountability for taking action. His peers on the team were becoming exceedingly frustrated, since their work was often held up because he had not delivered on his commitments.

Camastral started coaching him, giving him direct feedback, such as, "You said you would do this, but nothing happened. Let's talk about why." During one coaching session, Camastral sat down with the individual and gave him three concrete examples of instances in which he had failed to come through for the team and the negative consequences that had resulted. Lightning finally struck or, as the executive later told Camastral, "the conversation felt like a bee sting."

Once Camastral got the executive's attention, he invested time with him to illustrate the linkage between technical contributions and achieving sales and earnings growth, and to provide tips on how to contribute faster and more effectively. Before long, this team member became a significant contributor, accomplishing 5 to 10 times more work than ever before. "Even if I had had to spend 10 times longer to turn him around, it would have been worth it," says Camastral. "There is nothing more important than achieving the breakthrough."

Entire teams can turn a collective deaf ear to feedback, just as individual team members can. Paul Parker, currently chief people officer for Deloitte U.S., was once vice president of HR responsible for Colgate-Palmolive's Africa–Middle East Division. Parker recalls the problems the company had at one time with its South African subsidiary, which was considered by New York headquarters to be a team of mavericks.

South Africa was an independent business unit, a $150 million business run by functional VPs who were very successful at delivering results but often rode roughshod over one another and others in the organization, especially those in manufacturing. Although frequently called on the carpet by headquarters, the team's deaf ear led it to continue to engage in behaviors that violated global company policy.

Fortunately, the general manager realized that what was good for South Africa was not necessarily good for the rest of the organization, and that unless the subsidiary cleaned up its act it was never going to be viewed as world class and a source of global talent. With team survival hanging in the balance, Parker and the general manager of the subsidiary decided it was time for action. Says Parker:

We met with the whole team, and the GM led the initial discussion. He made a persuasive business case for change. The South African market could only grow so fast, he explained. The real way to achieve growth was to become a global supplier for C-P, and the only way to do this was to be viewed within the company as reliable global citizens. South Africa could no longer be the wild, wild West.

The group went through a "should be/as is" exercise, in which corporate values and expectations were placed alongside the team's actual values and behaviors. The disconnect became readily apparent. It dawned on everyone that delivering bottom-line results was important, but so was the way the team went about achieving them.

Following this exercise and alignment sessions, the team made the necessary behavioral changes. Before long, South Africa went from being a top-20 subsidiary to a top-5 subsidiary—one of the fastest growing in the corporation. The parent company made major investments in it, enabling it to become a global supplier of dental cream and a test bed for new-product toothpaste trials. Once considered mavericks who could not be trusted, many of the team members were promoted to major positions in the global company: The GM became CFO of North America, the company's biggest division; the controller went to Canada, a top-5 subsidiary, to become its financial controller; the HR person became head of HR for the U.K. As Parker sums it up, "They became a source of power because of their willingness to listen to feedback and act on it."

■ *Difficulty changing personal behavior*

Earlier in this chapter, we talked about self-awareness as the first step in behavior change. Before players can begin to replace dysfunctional, conflict-ridden relationships with healthy ones, they need to be aware of where their behavior falls on the continuum from nonassertive to assertive to aggressive. But awareness does not guarantee behavior change. In fact, changing one's interpersonal behavior is often the biggest obstacle a team member will face on the road to high performance.

Paul Parker has personally helped several executives over this hurdle. Parker recalls serving on a team that was dominated by one very aggressive executive. The team leader was new, as were some of the other team members. Constantly pointing out his own wealth of experience, this particular executive dismissed the others' opinions as uninformed. As a result, most of the team's decisions were being made from a single perspective, and the business began to suffer. The business unit was at risk of missing its targets, sales spiraling downward, and costs increasing.

Parker was also new to the team, but that did not stop him from confronting the executive about his aggressive behavior. After gathering feedback from each member of the team, Parker arranged a one-on-one meeting with the dominant executive, explaining why he needed to become less aggressive and more collaborative. "I let the facts speak for themselves," explains Parker. "I pointed out how alienated others felt when he refused to take their opinions seriously. He was bright; he got it right away. We made a pact. I suggested that when he felt the urge to take someone to task or to cut them off in a meeting, he should bite his tongue, call on me, and allow me to handle the situation more diplomatically. After I did this a few times, he began to see the value in treating people with more respect. Once he changed his behavior, we became a real team. And we started to get results: Sales went up; we got costs under control; we actually exceeded our target for profitable growth."

The Player as Coach

Not all team members are created equal. Joe Pieroni, president and CEO of Daiichi Sankyo Inc., says that this became apparent during his senior team's first alignment session. "By the end of those two days," he observes, "you know just who is going to need more time and more skill-based coaching in order to be successful."

As we explained in Chapter 2, Pieroni quickly arranged for his team to go through several skill-development workshops soon after their alignment, and he looked for opportunities for the team to apply their new learning in real time. Coaching was the third prong in his three-pronged approach. In keeping with his role as a high-performing leader, Pieroni carried out some of the coaching himself. But much of the coaching responsibility, for both enhancing skills and changing mindset, was shared with his team.

That a player is *duty bound* to serve as a coach to his or her peers is another radical change in mindset for many. It is part of the high-performance ascent up the Accountability Ladder. Paul Michaels recalls how his team members used to deal with their peers' deficiencies. "Before," comments Michaels, "they assumed it was my problem. Members of my staff would see other team members struggling and point it out to me." Michaels has seen a major shift since team members began holding themselves accountable for one another's performance. "Now, as a high-performing team," he reflects, "they automatically begin helping someone who is having trouble. They might give me a heads-up, but they try to help one another right away."

Helen McCluskey, president, Warnaco Intimate Apparel and Swimwear Group, has developed a number of great teams and great organizations using the high-performing team model. She likes to use sports analogies to describe the interactions of players on a great business team. "On a football team," she tells people, "if somebody misses a block, somebody else comes in to get it. The other members of the team don't just stand there and say, 'Joe missed that block. We lost.' It's the same way in business. If you see a team member who is falling down or struggling, you cannot be an observer; you have to help that person. At the end of the day, we are going to win or lose as a team, not as a collection of individuals."

One of the hallmarks of a great business team is the willingness of team members to assume accountability for the success of their colleagues. This can take many forms, from tough questioning to providing resources to coaching. While team members need not pretend to be professional coaches—nor should a player spend time trying to become one—members of great teams play an important coaching role, which is why we address what is arguably the thorniest coaching issue: how to deal with team members who are nearly or fully uncoachable.

Uncoachable or Just Tough to Coach?

Here is the $64 million question facing many, many teams: Is a team member who fails to initially respond to coaching uncoachable or just tough to coach?

Players resist change for many reasons. Some do not see "What's in it for me?"; others disagree on the need for change; still others are distrustful and ask, "What's the real agenda here?" There are those who are unclear about what the end state of change would look like for them. And then there are those who shy away from their discomfort zones. The challenge is to part the curtain to see what is behind the resistance to change.

Intention here is paramount. Is a team member's intention to change stronger than the lure of remaining comfortable with past ways of operating?

We once worked with a recently appointed CFO whose new job required him to speak confidently before investor groups. He was introverted and feared public speaking. But rather than get stuck in the "That's who I am; I've never done that before" story, he focused on "How do I do that?" and "What would it look like for me to succeed?" The CFO's intention was to show up as a confident public presenter. And, while he never became a Tony Robbins, the CFO's intention, combined with skills training, was enough to propel him forward well beyond previous limitations.

In another case, the top team of a major consumer goods manufacturer was having serious difficulties with one of its members, a newly appointed marketing executive with a retail background and a chronic need to be the center of attention. He felt that the transition to consumer goods would be a cakewalk, so he did not bother to master the basics. For him, team meetings were opportunities to strut his stuff, challenge the leader, and dominate discussion. Inevitably, his arrogance led to poor performance, but he refused to acknowledge his shortcomings.

The team leader initially confronted the situation head on, but to no avail. He next turned to several of the team players, asking them to provide coaching support to their faltering marketing colleague. They could not penetrate the executive's defensive armor either. In the end, the executive was terminated. The group president and team leader concluded that, "Sometimes, even on a high-performing team, you can only work at it for so long before you conclude that the person opts not to let go of an unproductive story and change."

The mind is a powerful ally—or foe—in one's coachability, as these contrasting examples attest. And, while leaders are ultimately responsible for making the call on the coachability of their players, every team member has an obligation to turn the tables on him- or herself by asking: Am I up to the task of continually reinventing myself to meet ever-more-demanding performance standards?

Self-diagnosis is a tricky business, but we have seen players engage in it with great candor and effectiveness. They begin by checking out the stories rattling around in their heads, asking themselves: "What are the conversations I'm having with myself?" and "Are any of them core limiting beliefs—stories that get in the way of what I profess to want?"

For example, had the CFO who feared public speaking hung onto the story, "I'm inherently shy and can't speak before groups," he would have fallen victim to a core limiting belief. But, like other successful executives who have put their stories behind them, the CFO was able to step back and become a dispassionate observer of his story. Such people are able to look at their stories like so much teletype at the bottom of a news channel. They become, in effect, third-party observers who realize that their stories do not run them. It is they who command—and are able to change—their stories in order to progress to the next level of performance.

What Are the Telltale Signs of Uncoachability?

It is the ultimate high-stakes moment for the members of a team: Sitting in their midst is an uncoachable player, or so they suspect. What are the telltale signs of uncoachability? How do you go about exploring below the surface? What are the ground rules? And when—and how—do you cut the cord?

These are not merely theoretical questions. A player's career and sense of well-being can hang in the balance, and the morale and effectiveness of the rest of the team and the player's function are likely to suffer. Here are a few tips, gained from hard-fought experience, to help separate the uncoachable from the merely tough to coach and to achieve success with even the most challenging cases.

Lesson One: When it comes to dealing with the uncoachable, timeliness is crucial. The sooner the team can make the call, the better for everyone involved. The organization saves time and money, and the player is spared the agony of trying to do the undoable. That is why it is often best to turn the coaching over to an external, professional coach who can form an objective picture and who will not hesitate to recommend swift action. But even if the team members elect to continue coaching the individual themselves or to engage one of their own HR staff, the decision needs to be made quickly.

In our experience, truly uncoachable individuals have been the exception, and, try as they might to conceal it, these individuals often reveal themselves during the coach's first encounter with them—if not sooner.

Data are the raw material of coaching. A good coach always begins by collecting data from the rest of the team and the team leader; the player's boss, if different from the team leader; his or her peers outside the team; and his or her direct reports. These data provide the initial clues that indicate the degree to which the person will respond to coaching. One of the best data-collecting questions to ask up front is: What specific behaviors point to the team member's need for coaching? Next, drill down further, especially if you suspect difficulty:

- Has the team member gone through prior, unsuccessful attempts at coaching, perhaps by the organization's HR professionals?
- Does the person have a reputation for being unable to accept criticism or for being completely intractable?
- Are the rest of the team, the team leader, and the player's sponsor, or internal mentor, truly committed to supporting him or her?
- Has the person engaged in "acting out" or exhibited abnormal behavior in the presence of other team members?

"Yes" answers to the first two questions are red-flag indicators that success of this assignment is iffy, as is a "no" answer to the third. A "yes" answer to the fourth question suggests that it is time for a psychiatrist or psychologist rather than an executive coach.

When Do You Press the "Eject" Button?

Here's the great Rubicon of coaching: Once you determine that a player is *unwilling to change,* there is little else that can be done. You have entered the uncoachable zone. As for players who are *willing but unable* to change, they too need to be given the news as soon as you recognize their uncoachability.

David Epstein, president and CEO of Novartis Oncology, has had to remove players who could not make the shift to the high-performance model, and he stresses that it is a responsibility that the team must share with the leader. Every team he has led, including the present one, has gone through business results at each of its meetings; if an area of the business was under-performing, its leader was questioned in detail. If the team was not satisfied with the answer, its members coached the person on how to get the data and bring back an action plan to resolve the issue. If, even after the coaching, the person was not capable of mobilizing his or her functional team to get back on track, he or she did not remain in the company.

For example, some years back, Epstein had a head of business devel-opment and licensing who was not able to bring in licensed products to supplement the company's own offerings. Licensing was core to the com-pany's growth strategy, and the senior team repeatedly tried to ascertain why efforts were not succeeding and to coach him toward success. "This individual's response," says Epstein, "was always that others were not giving him enough support, were not available, were not doing the right analysis, were not dedicating their people to the due-diligence teams. It became apparent to everyone that this person just wasn't willing to be candid or to take responsibility for results, and he was asked to leave."

Epstein points out that this has never happened on his current team—whose members he hand-picked because they had the mindset and skills required to serve on a great business team.

TESTING COACHABILITY

How coachable are the players on your team? Here are eight questions to test a person's coachability when faced with the need to change:

1. Is the team member focused on the future or stuck in the past? (Can the person envision what a "happy ending" would look like? How he/she would show up differently?)
2. Does the person listen to the rationale for change rather then defend the *status quo*?

(Continued)

TESTING COACHABILITY *(Continued)*

3. Do the player's discussions revolve around his or her intent to change and how to make it happen, or does he/she continue to debate the need to do so?
4. Is the person able to step back and take a depersonalized look at him/herself and his/her situation?
5. Is the player willing to let go of core limiting beliefs and stories?
6. Does the team member clearly see the positive consequences for change? Does he/she see higher payoffs for change versus the costs of remaining stuck in past "stories"?
7. Does the person express willingness to partner with a coach on the journey forward?
8. Has the intention to change been converted into an action plan—and do results mirror that intention?

Player Imperative: Raise the Bar

Just as great leaders continually raise the performance bar for themselves and their teams, members of great business teams do the very same.

When Cathy Burzik's team at Applied Biosystems encouraged her to spend more time on strategic issues, telling her in effect to leave the driving of operations to members of the team, they willingly sought and accepted greater responsibility for running the business. This freed up Burzik's time to focus on strategic issues and enabled team members to take on greater challenges and raise their level of play.

And as is true with just about every other great business team we have seen, the results were impressive and the top team's behavior became infectious. Applied Biosystems soon made its first two acquisitions in many years, and Burzik's high-performing team enabled her to spend much of her remaining time at AB identifying and assessing additional opportunities for growth. "Our team kept raising the bar, acting more and more like owners of the company," Stevenson recalls. "The culture that was created by that shift required that the bar also be raised for the next level down, so they could take up the day-to-day responsibilities and allow us to focus on the bigger issues."

End Thought

When teams are first introduced to high-performance concepts, they typically do not turn cartwheels of enthusiasm at the prospect of becoming "great." There is noticeable skepticism—even anxiety—in the air.

Recently, we conducted a three-city video conference with the top team and those reporting to it—a total of about 50 executives—at Fonterra Co-operative Group Limited in Australia. The new managing director of the Australia-New Zealand business unit, John Doumani, called the conference to initiate the project, designed to create a horizontal organization and great business teams within it. Despite Doumani's attempts to stimulate discussion, there were few questions and comments from the participants. Their reluctance brought to mind a comment that Linda Scard Buitenhek, former VP cleansing platform, skin care for Johnson & Johnson's consumer products company, once made about the early stage of the journey toward great business teams: "People hate it before they love it." Scard should know. She has seen many teams evolve from initial skepticism to the unbridled enthusiasm that comes from the solid success and élan of being on a team of high-performing players.

This, incidentally, is exactly what Doumani pointed out to his team. "Before long," he told the executives participating in the video conference, "each of you will discover how liberating it is be a high-performance player in a horizontal organization." He too should know. Doumani has led great teams in three other major organizations that he has helped to transform.

We know of no great team leader who has ever felt that his or team had reached the end of its journey to high performance. It is just one more example of great leaders and teams setting ambitious, stretch goals for themselves. But it is possible to accelerate the move from the current level of performance to a significantly higher one. How do great teams accomplish this? That is the subject of our next chapter: Aligning for High Performance.

Notes

1. For complete survey results, see: Howard Guttman and Andrew Longman, "Project Teams: How Good Are They?" *Quality Progress,* February 2006.
2. For a full explanation of the process of assessing where others stand and the best ways in which to influence them, see Appendix B.
3. The Thomas-Kilmann Conflict Mode Instrument, figure B.2 in Appendix B, is a graphic representation of these five methods.

4

Aligning for High Performance

- At one time Redken Fifth Avenue was a lackluster brand. Once #1 in the professional beauty industry, it had slipped to #3 or #4. Younger customers thought of Redken as "what my mother used." Internally, the company was highly siloed, with Sales and Education—the latter being the department that trains hairdressers to use Redken products—constantly at loggerheads. There was no clear agreement between them as to who was supposed to be doing what or where one group's responsibility ended and the other's began. Important tasks began to fall through the cracks. Today, Redken has had 10 years of double-digit sales and profit growth, unmatched by any of its competitors. The company receives constant positive feedback about the quality of its people, programs, and way of doing business. Competitors even join in, saying, "We're sick and tired of hearing customers tell us to do it the way Redken does."

- Pfizer's acquisition of Warner–Lambert's (WL) consumer healthcare business in 2000 created a number of challenges for its merged Sales Department. Three years later, many of these were still unresolved: leaders without the necessary competencies; legacy Pfizer employees lined up on one side of decisions and former WL folks on the other, with both sides refusing to budge; lack of collaboration with Marketing, and so on. In 2003, the department had its lowest top-line sales and revenue since the merger. By 2004, the divide had been completely bridged. As team members stopped viewing themselves as "Pfizer" or "WL," decision making gained momentum. Sales and Marketing were working together so seamlessly they were like one group. In 2004 and 2005 the team blew away its plan on both the top and bottom lines. And Pfizer Consumer won more vendor-of-the-year awards from its customers than any of its competitors—beating P&G to become number one in 2005.

- In 2002, Philip Morris USA's IT organization was an underperformer. It completed only 35 major projects a year, and only 60% of these were on time and on budget. On a scale of 1 to 5, internal client satisfaction was rated 2.5, and IT was told it needed to improve the way it managed projects and to align its goals and priorities with the rest of the company. One year later, the same organization completed over 70 major projects, 85% of which were on time and on budget. Internal client satisfaction scores had risen from 2.5 to 4. To top it all off, PMUSA was not merely selected as one of *ComputerWorld*'s "100 Best Places to Work in IT" for the first time ever, but it placed an impressive 14th on the list.

Put yourself and your team in the middle of any one of these situations. Would you have risen to the occasion? And would you and your team, like the ones just cited, have been able to leverage the challenge into a new way of operating—one that made meeting the "challenges beyond the challenge" a matter of business routine?

The Redken, Pfizer, and Philip Morris USA teams did not reinvent themselves overnight or without effort. Each team had a leader who was keenly aware of the magnitude of the challenge, who avoided business-as-usual fixes in favor of a high-performance, horizontal solution, and who transformed the challenge into a "burning platform" for moving his team to action. This chapter provides a window into how ordinary, mediocre teams have accelerated their performance to become great.

The Four Stages of Team Development: From Hierarchical to Horizontal

Think about a business team that you are either leading or on which you are currently a member. It does not matter much whether your team is facing a crisis situation or relative calm. Teams tend to face all situations with the same basic behavioral repertoire. After glancing at the Team Development Wheel (Figure 4.1), in which quadrant would you locate your team?

Without knowing your team, here is a safe prediction: Unless your team has undertaken a serious effort to transform itself along the lines suggested in this book, it is either in Stage 1 or Stage 2.

We have never met a great business team—one with the attributes listed under Stage 4—that operated in that quadrant from day one. Every great team works its way through at least three stages as it accelerates to high performance.

The notion of "stages" of team development is somewhat parallel to the stages of historical development propounded by many thinkers as far back as Plato. Our use of the concept is meant to describe four observable behavioral clusters that characterize teams as they go about the tasks of solving problems and making decisions. But there is no sense of inevitability implied by the four stages of development. You do not necessarily move constantly forward around the wheel, even with effort and the best of intentions. Some teams remain stuck in Stage 1 or 2; others progress to Stages 3 and 4 only to stall and regress.

There are no hard-and-fast boundaries separating the stages. Teams are human constructs and, as such, are not given to clean-cut conceptual delineations. Nevertheless, walk into a Stage 1 team meeting and you can feel the heavy atmospherics, the weariness, the lack of authentic give-and-take, the tabling or even denial of conflict, and the looking to the leader for decision cues. Walk into a Stage 4 meeting and you can sense the high voltage of a team that is firmly performance oriented, riveted on getting things done, unafraid to enter each other's turf, and that has a leader seated in every chair around the table.

Time spent together is a key variable in the development of a team. Most newly formed teams spend most, if not all, of their time in Stage 1.

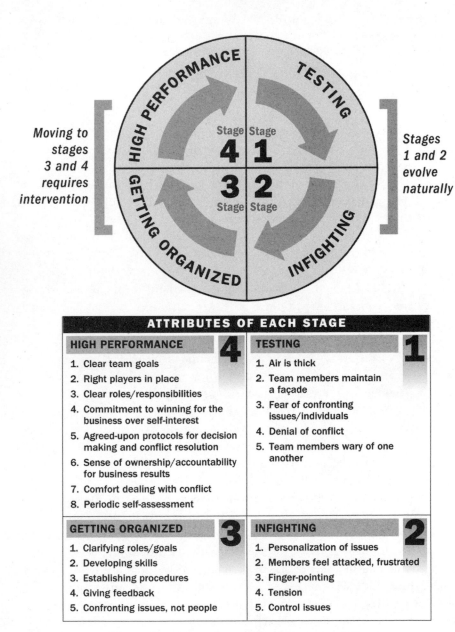

Figure 4.1   The Team Development Wheel

If the players have not worked together closely before, they tend to shy away from confrontational behavior. "Niceness" prevails, although there is a palpable undercurrent of tension most of the time.

But this is not always true. Some players may be highly aggressive, or there may be issues that they feel so strongly about that confrontation erupts every so often. At such times, the team moves briefly into Stage 2, then retreats back to Stage 1.

In contrast, long-standing intact teams tend to bounce back and forth between Stages 1 and 2. Over the years, they have adopted a number of dysfunctional behaviors, which guide interactions between and among players. Old grudges linger. Cliques and factions line up predictably on issues. Feedback is viewed as feed*attack*. But they may also retreat to Stage 1 from time to time. Tired of counterproductive infighting, adversaries may temporarily go underground to enlist supporters for the next round.

However often teams may naturally move between Stages 1 and 2, our many years of observation have convinced us of this: *It is a rare team that can accelerate to Stage 3 without outside intervention.* The attributes that players require in these stages do not come naturally. As we have seen, the personal transformations that leaders and players must go through are difficult and uncomfortable. They require commitment, courage, and a disciplined process.

The goal, or "should be," is to embody the eight attributes of a Stage 4 team. If your team is not yet there, even if it is committed to fundamentally changing its level of play, there is only one way to accelerate its progress around the Team Development Wheel: Your team must become a fully aligned entity.

Alignment: From Concept to Action

When a team is clear and committed to a common direction, when it focuses on business deliverables that evolve from that direction, when it is clear about its roles and responsibilities, when decision-making protocols are in place, and when business relationships are open and avoid siloism, then it acquires new performance muscle and the will to win. This is what we mean by "getting aligned."

Aligning a business team is a disciplined, phased process that moves along a path from seeing with clarity and precision the "as is" of its behavior, to rebuilding its architecture and behavior patterns, to accelerating to high performance, and, finally, to making that higher level of performance the future "as is."

The alignment process is made up of two phases: *Making the Diagnosis* and *Gaining Agreement*. Our discussion of these phases provides a street-level, detailed view of the alignment process. You do not move a team along the path to becoming great without touching every facet of individual and team behavior. The details and examples we provide are intended to give you a full appreciation of what alignment entails and what to expect in moving your team out of Stage 1 or 2.

Phase 1: Making the Diagnosis

Think of this first phase as the "sunshine" phase of the process. The objective is to shine a bright light on the team so that it gains a clear, comprehensive view of how the team behaves as it solves problems, makes decisions, plans, and conducts its business. This phase pinpoints the team's coordinates on the Team Development Wheel.

Taking Stock   The impetus to form a great business team typically starts with the leader and his or her need to overcome a pressing business challenge. That challenge often prompts a leader to reflect on the team's readiness to respond. What emerges from this deep-think is the realization that a wide gap exists between the "as is" and the "should be" of team performance, and that now is the time to make fundamental changes.

Whether the team leader is the CEO, a division president, a general manager, or a functional head, here is the basic question that he or she must address at the outset: *What would the team look like if it could be taken to the next level of performance?* And then: What would the higher-performing team be able to accomplish? What goals would it be able to reach? What barriers would no longer exist? What problems would be solved?

Wise leaders do not attempt to answer these questions alone. Here is where a trusted consultant can play an important role. As the leader answers these questions, the consultant must help keep the leader's analysis sharp and grounded to avoid either unrealistic wish-listing or minimalist thinking that will lock the team into business as usual.

Engaging the Team No matter how benignly it is packaged, the message from the leader that "We need to up the performance bar" is implicitly disquieting. It puts the *status quo* on trial. This is why the next step toward alignment is so critical. It is here that the leader communicates with his or her team members, allays their fears, secures buy-in, and generates excitement for the new world of significantly higher performance.

During this overview session, which generally runs between 1½ and 2 hours, the leader begins by presenting the business case for a performance-improvement initiative, "We are here, and we need to be there." This is the time for the leader to share his or her initial perspective on the situation.

At Australia-based Fonterra, John Doumani, managing director, Fonterra Australia-New Zealand, launched the initial briefing on becoming a high-performance organization by reflecting on his first four months with his new company. In his remarks to his top 50 players, he pointed to the strategic and operational challenges the company faced in growing a global business, the need to improve the top and bottom revenue lines, the challenge of rationalizing the business, a   nd the need to unleash the brain-power of everyone in the organization. "To get there," he added, "we need the rigor of an alignment process and professional coaching support."

Effective leaders come with solutions, not just problem statements. At the initial team meeting, the leader must drive home the connection between alignment and high performance. Doumani did just that. He painted a clear, straightforward, and animated picture of what the high-performance end game implied for everyone attending the briefing. "When the eight attributes of a high-performance team are in place," he declared confidently, "you'll never want to work anywhere else." That statement got his team's attention.

Doumani next raised the question: How much energy does it take you to do your job? "Given the way we function, way too much," he volunteered. "Why? Because it takes much more energy to work *around* issues than to work *through* them."

Doumani put meat on all this by translating his vision into expected performance outcomes that result from operating at high-performing levels: "Once-daunting stretch targets for revenue and profitability will seem like low-hanging fruit; product development time will be cut in half; we'll proact rather than merely react to the competition; making decisions— especially the energy-draining ones related to resource allocation—will be much easier; key projects will be delivered on time, on budget, and on plan." And for the kicker: Doumani promised his team that moving to the new model would not diminish the top team's power. Rather, it would *increase* it by better leveraging resources.

While during this session the leader presents the "what" and "why" of alignment, it is the consultant's job to brief the team on the "how"—the steps going forward in the alignment process.

Finally, there needs to be a segue to data collection, the next phase of alignment and team transformation. Team members need to be informed that the consultant will be speaking individually with each of them to get their perspectives on the gap between the way things are and the way they ought to be.

Getting the Facts   The alignment process is a team effort. Do team members share the leader's view of the situation? Do they share the same sense of urgency and a similar assessment of the barriers to high performance? It is up to the consultant to draw out and analyze the many viewpoints and "stories" that lie beneath the surface.

Confidentiality is an imperative, allowing team members to answer candidly a series of tough questions that cover the team's current degree of alignment in the five key areas.

We suggest using an ascending scale of 1 to 5 to capture responses to questions such as:

- From "not clear" to "very clear," how would you rate the clarity of team goals?
- From "not clear" to "very clear," how clear are you about your role/accountability on the team? Others' roles/accountabilities?
- From "wary, closed, with hidden agendas" to "candid, open, relaxed, easy to speak your mind," how would you rate the working atmosphere within the team?
- From "rarely" to "always," how often are decisions made according to an agreed-upon set of protocols?

- Do team members work together independently or interdependently?
- How effective is the team, *operating as a team*, in accomplishing its business goals?

Along with this set of quantitative questions, some open-ended questions, designed to obtain qualitative data, are also asked. For example:

- What are some of the things that are not working in the way the team functions? What *is* working?
- What would it take for the team to achieve a "5" on effectiveness?
- What one suggestion would you give your team leader to increase his or her effectiveness in this position?
- What is the major obstacle that is preventing/could prevent you from fulfilling your role on the team as effectively as possible?
- Where on the team is greater interdependence needed?

At the end of these 45- to 60-minute individual interviews, the consultant has an accurate picture of how long and difficult the journey to alignment is going to be, and that information is shared first with the team leader, then with the rest of the team.

Giving the Leader a Heads-Up　　Some leaders perceive the feedback from their team as a personal challenge or, worse, an attack. If that is the case, the consultant can add value by working with the leader to depersonalize the critique and view it as facts presented in a business case. This is an important learning moment for the leader. He or she must understand that accepting such feedback, however disturbing the news, is essential for progress. And it is equally important for team members, who perhaps for the first time have expressed themselves candidly, even if their feedback comes cloaked in anonymity.

As Chico's Edmonds explains, "I don't know any senior executive who enjoys being told that he or she doesn't walk on water. But once you get over the shock, you can then move on to considering the feedback from your team and improving your leadership ability—and the abilities of those on your team."

The consultant must give the leader a chance to absorb the team's feedback before going public with it, not just as a courtesy, but to enable the two to plan the next step in the alignment process. Together, they discuss which of the five key alignment areas will require the most work, where the strategy is unclear or poorly understood, where there is confusion over roles, where there appear to be breakdowns between individual players, where turf battles between functions seem to be paralyzing the team, where decision making is stalled, which team members are perceived as either aggressive or nonassertive by their peers, and so on. Think of the one-hour heads-up session with the leader as the "choreographing" of the actual alignment session—which is the next step in the process.

Phase 2: Gaining Agreement

During this phase the consultant presents the team with an accurate reflection of itself—by "holding up the mirror." The alignment session is held, during which new patterns of behavior in the five key areas are agreed on.

Holding up the Mirror   The team-alignment session is an intensive, two-day experience. The first order of business is to have the team take a good, long look in the mirror. It is not always a pretty reflection. For many, this is the first honest look they have ever had at themselves as individuals and team players. This is the time for the leader and consultant to share with the entire team the consolidated data from the interviews that were conducted during Phase 1.

As an example, here are the consolidated numerical responses to three questions, along with a representative sampling of comments, from the members of a senior, global team in the pharmaceutical industry.

1. Clarity of team business goals (focus/priorities):

| *Responses:* | | 2 | 1 | 3 | 1 | 7 | |
| Not Clear | 1 | 2 | 3 | 4 | 5 | | Very Clear |

1a. Top priorities for this team for the next 12 months:
- Deliver this year's numbers.
- Accelerate growth through innovation; increase pace and quality.
- Establish platform for accelerated growth in emerging markets.
- Drive costs out of system to enable accomplishment of the above.

The responses to these questions were very encouraging. Unlike many teams in Stage 1 or Stage 2, this one had an excellent understanding of what the larger organization expected from it. Unfortunately, when it came to delivering on those goals, the outcome was far less promising.

2. Effectiveness of the team operating as a team in accomplishing its business goals:

Responses:	**1**	**5**	**2**	**5**	
Not Clear	1	2	3	4	5	Very Clear

2a. What would it take to be a "5"?
- Become a global, rather than a siloed team.
- Be more collaborative, less competitive. We are incredibly objective driven, and the objectives against which we are measured promote siloed behavior.
- Eliminate perception of an *inner* group and an *outer* group: seems like most key decisions are made by the "in" group.
- Greater transparency among players—real issues don't come up (e.g., how the team operates, individual player performance).
- Need clear process for decision making and escalating decisions.
- Team leader allows people to approach him individually after meetings and overturns decisions made in meetings.
- Head of Europe is seen by many team members as a barrier to creating a collaborative, transparent environment. He is viewed as abrasive, oppositional . . . .
- Etc.

With none of the players rating their effectiveness higher than a 3, this team was definitely in trouble. The answers to the open-ended questions indicate a group of individuals whose lack of cohesion was clearly impeding their ability to meet their goals.

3. Working atmosphere within the team:

Responses:		**4**	**3**	**2**	**2**	**2**		Candid/open/
Wary, closed,								relaxed; easy
Hidden agendas	1	2		3		4	5	to speak your mind

3a. Issues impacting openness:
- Concern regarding team leader's responses if team members are honest in their opinions.
- Competitive nature of team, lack of substantive relationships, pay-for-performance structure.
- Perception that there are inner/outer groups.
- Head of Europe's perceived unwillingness to align with the team and the resulting reluctance to make suggestions/challenge him.
- Individual agendas (e.g., lack of trust in head of Europe's numbers;
- Etc.

Here again, the majority of the players gave themselves low ratings on their ability to express themselves freely and to disagree with one another and the leader. No candor and no trust equal no results.

Although at least one individual on this team was highly aggressive, and some people responded to him with Stage 2 behavior—public arguments, frustration, and anger—the scores and comments indicate clearly that this team spent most of its time in Stage 1.

Most of the players were obviously intimidated by the head of Europe and also by the team leader. There had been significant churn among the players and, as one of the comments indicates, some of the newer people were reluctant to voice their opinions. The air was definitely "thick."

Back in Chapter 1, we enumerated the five factors that all great business teams have in common:

1. A high-performance leader who, among other things, models the right behavior, builds authentic relationships, and empowers players to become leaders as well
2. *Us*-directed players whose focus is on the team, not their own function or interests
3. Protocols for decision making and conflict resolution
4. Continual attention to raising the bar for the entire team
5. A supportive performance management system

This team, like most Stage 1 teams, did not even come close:

1. Its leader role-modeled all the wrong behaviors: allowing team members to triangulate, not sharing decision-making power, playing favorites, winning through intimidation, and so on.
2. There was no sense of "us" among the players. The team was really no more than a group of managers, representing different geographical regions, who met occasionally to discuss some—but certainly not all—of the information needed to run the business. Each competed for resources, for attention from the leader, and for power.
3. There was no clear process for making or escalating decisions. Decisions were made in full group, then rescinded by the leader, who caved in to pressure from those who disagreed. Conflict was settled according to the "might makes right" school of resolution.
4. The team was well aligned on its goals: meeting this year's numbers; raising the bar; accelerating growth, especially in emerging areas; and driving down costs:
5. Rather than being rewarded for achieving the team's goals, players were rewarded for results in their region, making competition the byword on the team.

One factor out of five—a long way to go.

The effect of such self-reflection is very powerful, as Gerard Kells, vice president, HR, operations and technology for Johnson & Johnson, can attest:

When the team sees the data, they realize that it's theirs: They own it; it describes them. They realize that they all agree on the importance of functioning well as a team, and they all agree that they're not doing it. Sitting in the group, having the data fed back to you, you find out that everyone else thinks the same way you do. But nobody has ever talked about it openly before. All of sudden, everyone's true feelings have been let out, and there's no denying them, no taking them back. It's sobering—and a little frightening as well.

With a clear picture of the team's behavior in hand, it is now time to confront head on the issues that have been unearthed. The consultant asks team members to look objectively at the data, treating it as a business case in which they have no personal stake. It is helpful to divide the team into small groups, with each one considering four questions—three based on the data and the fourth on gut feeling:

1. What are some of the adjectives that you would use to describe this team?
2. What is the main message, or story, that comes through about this team?
3. What are the obvious issues that this team needs to resolve?
4. What will happen to this team if, five months from now, it has not changed?

The groups then reassemble to share their responses. In the case of the senior pharmaceutical team, here are the answers its members gave:

1. *Adjectives*: siloed, insecure, angry, frustrated, individual performance-driven, individualistic, subeffective, numbers-driven, colluding, exclusionary—and hopeful.
2. *Main messages:*
   - Despite years of globalization, team still works in silos.
   - Team wants to reinvent itself, to transform the industry, but is it ready?
   - There is a broad split on most questions; this Dr. Jekyll and Mr. Hyde team needs to get its act together.
   - The team is clear on many fronts, woefully short on others.
   - We are hopeful about the future.
   - Etc.

3. *Issues that need to be resolved:*
   We need to:
   - build deeper, more constructive, and respectful collaborations.
   - break down existing barriers to communication.
   - ensure the commitment of all to the overall business strategy.
   - make decision making more inclusive.
   - team versus regional success.
   - change the performance system reward
   - Etc.
4. *What will happen if we do not change?*
   We will:
   - not make the numbers that have been set for us.
   - fail to grow the market.
   - miss opportunities to gain market share.
   - continue to see team members fail.
   - never reach our its full potential.
   - Etc.

The activities we have just described are not academic exercises or simulated bonding experiences. They are a tough-minded, often gut-wrenching first step in changing the way teams think about themselves. For what is often the first time, individual team members see themselves without the cosmetics and camouflage. They begin to understand the implications of their own behaviors on that of the group. They begin to realize exactly how much is at stake. And they begin to buy into the need to change.

Discussion now centers on the fact that high-performing teams—teams that score fours and fives on the questionnaire—are aligned in all five key areas, and this alignment is key to successfully working through conflict and attaining the expected business results.

It is time for the heavy lifting.

Holding the Alignment Session   We have already said that there are *five key areas* in which the team needs to be aligned:

1. Business strategy
2. Business deliverables coming from the strategy

3. Roles and responsibilities at individual and business unit or functional levels
4. Protocols, or ground rules, for decision making and conflict resolution
5. Business/interpersonal relationships/interdependencies

The end result of alignment in the first three areas is agreement among the players and their leader about *what* the team as a whole is going to accomplish and *what* each individual will contribute to those results. Alignment in the fourth and fifth areas deals with agreement about *how* the group is going to carry out its tasks and *how* the players and leaders are going to interact with one another.

The amount of time spent on each of the areas during the session depends on the data. If, as in the case of the senior pharmaceutical team we have been following, the consolidated data tell us that the team is very clear about its strategic mission and operational goals, then there is no need to fix what is not broken. We just move on to the areas that the data tell us are trouble spots.

While there is no sure way to predict where a team will need the most work, there are telltale indicators. The length of time that the team has been working together is one of the best predictors of potential trouble. On a newly formed team, gaining agreement on goals and roles is frequently a major focus during the alignment. On the positive side, "young" teams have not had a chance to develop the bad habits—and bad blood— that dog so many long-standing teams. The latter are usually reasonably clear about what they need to accomplish, but their long history of dysfunctional behavior keeps them from moving ahead.

Aligning with the Business Strategy   Strategic alignment entails fundamental agreement on the future direction of the business—the organization's competitive advantage, the products and markets the organization will offer and serve, as well as those that fall outside the boundary—the capabilities needed now and to go forward, and the longer-term growth and financial targets.

Fortunately for the senior pharmaceutical team we have been discussing, the corporation's leaders had formulated and communicated an exceedingly clear strategy for the overall organization and its component parts. Unfortunately, many teams do not have that advantage.

A number of years ago, the North American and European senior teams of a global consumer goods company met to set worldwide strategy. The North Americans championed the new strategy that emerged, while their European counterparts nodded in silent agreement but never really bought in. No sooner had the meeting concluded than both sides went back to their respective areas with mixed messages. This set off fierce competition for resources, with each area pursuing different product and marketing approaches. Within 18 months, the new-product pipeline was empty and time to market lagged 30% behind the industry standard.

This company found out the hard way that strategic misalignment leads to self-sabotage and forces senior management to spend time plugging leaks in the dike rather than working seamlessly to implement key priorities.

In contrast, the IT team at Philip Morris USA that we cited at the beginning of this chapter is fully aligned with corporate strategy. Since taking over the department, vice president of information services and CIO Joe Amado has taken great pains to improve the alignment between IT and the business. One of his efforts focused on developing a set of "visioning sessions," in which he brings together IT professionals and leaders of PMUSA's various businesses to discuss how to more tightly align their respective strategies. One strategic initiative coming from these sessions involved having Amado's team upgrade key systems in order to deliver real-time sales data to field reps. The team now produces daily updates on sales activities, such as the number of sales calls made and the number of stores contacted. "[IT] is giving us the tools to have a much more productive sales organization," Ross Webster, vice president of customer service and distribution at Philip Morris, reported. From a business unit, function, or department perspective, strategic alignment is primarily about knowing where your business adds greatest value and then setting your priorities accordingly. This was the point of Amado's visioning sessions. "The [IT] organization was looking for that road map of where we were going and why," according to Amado. "I wanted to make sure we were crystal clear on the value this [IT] organization delivers."[1]

The former president of a major consumer goods company that we worked with put a great deal of effort into ensuring that his team avoided the strategic misalignment trap. It worked. When his team discussed issues and opportunities, it always referred back to the strategy and the key performance indicators that it had developed. These were embedded in the team's thinking and behaviors.

According to the executive, "When you are all on the same page regarding the principles by which you want to drive the business—the values of the company and the quality of the results you want—these principles become your decision-making guide. All you have to do is ask, 'Is my choice in keeping with these principles?' If so, I can go on and make the decision and defend my view. If not, I have to choose differently." He says that the only question he ever asks about a decision is, "Is it consistent with our strategy?"

When we align a senior team, a great deal of time may be spent on getting agreement on strategy. At a minimum, a team should review the existing strategy to make sure that it is clear, that the assumptions remain valid, and that everyone remains committed to its execution.

As the alignment process cascades from the senior team, there is a need to test how well each team member at every level understands the strategy, is committed to it, and knows how the work of the team fits in.

Aligning Business Deliverables   How can you ensure that the day-to-day work your team is engaged in is supportive of organizational goals and values? It is not something you can take for granted. When a new CEO we know called together his senior team for the first time, he asked them how many open projects they had. They told him that there were 475 projects under way. His response: "Here are seven goals that will be driving the company and ensuring our alignment with corporate goals. How many of the 475 have anything to do with these seven goals?" They sheepishly answered that 33 of the 475 projects were in alignment with the goals he had articulated. The CEO responded, "Reassess the 442 nonstrategic projects!"

Joe Amado and his team have gone well beyond alignment between departmental and organizational strategy. Working side by side with the heads of various departments, they developed operational goals to support each department's respective business plan. Every quarter IT meets with line executives to find out how well it is delivering against strategic and project-specific objectives and supporting day-to-day operations.

To ensure that his team adds day-to-day value, Amado manages outside the box—literally. He has placed IT managers directly into the business divisions to better understand business requirements. He also encourages IT managers to transfer out of the technology area for a year or two to work in other divisions within the company.

Amado and his team are also working to improve business processes through the use of IT. While the processes are owned by business units (for example, supply chain management is overseen by the Logistics Department), IT is focused on how those processes work from an end-to-end systems perspective. The goal is continuous improvement. "I feel good about where we are today because of what I hear from our clients," says Amado. "Are we great? I think we're getting close."[2]

When David Greenberg, senior vice president of HR for L'Oréal USA, came into the job, L'Oréal was undergoing a major transition. The U.S. affiliate, including HR, had been operating very differently from the worldwide company, and the CEO decided that it was time to begin operating as a unified, integrated group. There were major implications on organization structure, processes, and systems.

Greenberg inherited an intact HR team that had been working together for many years. Corporate VPs of HR report directly to him. Each divisional VP of HR reports directly to a line boss and on a dotted line to Greenberg; they include the vice presidents of HR for the Professional Division, the Consumer Division, the Luxury Division, the Active Cosmetics Division, Manufacturing, Administration, and R&D. Each of these is a separate, large business unit or functional group with strong leaders, a disparate culture, and different objectives. Not surprisingly, there was no strong sense of a team or a shared destiny among the HR leaders. It was not an environment very conductive to developing across-the-organization objectives for the HR function, much less delivering against them.

Greenberg moved to improve the way his team worked together, especially in terms of communication, openness, sharing the same objectives, and holding each other accountable for results.

In order to align the team and establish clear common goals, Greenberg conducted a brief survey among the line bosses to understand both how they saw the Human Resources Department and what their expectations of it were. Their responses made it clear that they wanted the HR function to raise the bar and play a greater role in meeting the needs of the business. They also wanted greater input into key HR issues and a means to assess progress made. For the HR team, it quickly became evident that there was a great desire to be less tactical and to play a greater role in driving the company's overall results. The team was ready and excited to take on this new role.

Many actions were taken as a result of this alignment, including the centralization of certain activities that historically were the prerogative of each division, such as candidate sourcing, new-hire orientations, and leave administration. In addition, a set of consistent metrics was developed, and from it a "People P&L" was created to ensure that the team was looking at key indicators in the same way and basing its actions on them.

Perhaps the greatest accomplishment was the creation of a new spirit of collaboration, a sense of a shared mission, and the openness and trust required to tackle some of the thorniest HR issues. Greenberg described a recent meeting in which "the team was discussing some critical issues affecting talent retention and didn't hesitate to disagree with one other, put provocative ideas on the table, and in the end agree on one course of action, to which all committed fully."

Aligning Roles and Responsibilities   Whose job is it, anyhow? These are five of the most loaded words in the management lexicon. Unless you are crystal clear on the answer, count on turf battles and your organization becoming a house divided. Paul Michaels, president of Mars, Inc., describes some of the turf battles that typically occur when team players do not agree on the "Whose job is it, anyhow?" question:

> Efficiency drives Manufacturing, which explains that function's bias toward developing one product spec for all customers. Sales, on the other hand, is under pressure from significant clients to provide customized products. The VP of Sales promises the customized products, and his or her counterpart in Marketing encourages that group to begin advertising the variations. Sometimes R&D comes up with a complicated design that strains Manufacturing's resources. As complaints emerge, the VP of Manufacturing makes the call to change some of the specifications. Everyone is pulled in different directions, and, before you know it, it can be all-out war.

An organization at war with itself does not have much in reserve to fend off competitors or listen to its customers. Without aligned roles and responsibilities, it is difficult to imagine an organization remaining on top of its game, much less moving up to Stage 4 greatness.

Two of the prealignment questions that we ask players are designed to gauge the degree of work needed in this area: "How clear are you about *your* role/accountability on the team?" and "How clear are you about the *other team members'* roles/accountability?"

Here are the consolidated numeric and open-ended responses of the senior pharmaceutical team to these questions:

1. Your clarity about your role/accountability:

Responses:		1	1	4	8	
Not Clear	1	2	3	4	5	Very Clear

2. Your clarity about other players' roles/accountability

Responses:		1	3	3	4	2	
Not Clear	1	2		3	4	5	Very Clear

Comments:

- The role of Innovation is not clear to many team members: What is Andrew's [the head of this group's] mandate? What are his boundaries? How is he to interrelate with others on the team [e.g., Marketing and the regional heads]?
- What are the functional strategic directions of HR? R&D? Marketing?
- Who is responsible for delivering advertising spending across the board?

This team was fairly clear about roles and accountabilities, although there were a few areas of ambiguity. On teams where the responses indicate that there is considerable confusion in this area, we allocate a significant portion of the alignment session to clearing it up. For this, we need very specific data.

Here is an exercise we recommend you consider conducting to clear up role-and-responsibility confusion: Ask each member of your team to write his or her answers to the following questions on an easel sheet, then post the sheets on the conference-room wall.

1. What are your key responsibilities on this team?
2. What are the activities for which you are responsible?
3. With whom, on this team and outside it, do you need to collaborate to get your job done?
4. What do you think other players perceive your job on the team to be?
5. What questions do you have about your role on the team?

Then have each team member and the team leader move around the room to review each person's sheet, putting their initials next to each statement that they disagree with or have questions about. As each player's initials are added, the disconnects will become increasingly apparent.

In sessions we lead, we next discuss each disconnect. The objective is to assign each contested role or responsibility to one person. In keeping with the spirit of high-performing teams, everyone is encouraged to weigh in during the discussion. If after a reasonable time those directly involved cannot reach agreement, the leader steps in and makes the call. While this exercise takes time, when teams look back after the alignment they invariably believe it was well worth the investment.

Aligning Protocols   Here is how CEO Scott Edmonds describes the toughest struggle that he had as the leader of Chico's top team during the move to the high-performing team model:

> The hardest part of the transition was following the model all the way up to the point of terminating those who refused to abide by the new rules. One of the senior vice presidents on my team wasn't being honest with me and kept going underground. In the prealignment interviews, the other players made it clear that they believed she had to go. I realized that I had to terminate her

immediately or I wouldn't be playing it straight, and the day after the alignment, I asked her to leave. As a leader you must say, "Okay, these are the new rules of the game." To use a baseball analogy, it's like saying, "Three strikes and you're out is no longer the rule. It's now only two strikes." If I allow someone three strikes, I'm not playing by the rules and neither are they.

Whether or not you institute a "two strikes" policy is situational and beside the point. What is important is having in place—and sticking to— agreed-upon rules of behavior for handling contentious situations.

We call these rules "protocols," and they govern the way a team inter- acts on a day-to-day basis. Simple rules such as no triangulation or enlist- ment of third parties; resolve it or let it go; do not accuse in absentia; and no hands from the grave can eliminate much of the unresolved conflict and second-guessing that paralyze teams and keep them from moving to a higher level of performance.

During its alignment, Chico's top team agreed that underground behavior was no longer going to be tolerated. In the weeks and months after the alignment, sticking to that rule was not always easy, but it proved to be worth the effort, says Edmonds.

It was a difficult situation. Our HR executive left; our Marketing executive left; our heads of Real Estate and Stores left. There was a parade of people who left because they were not willing to play by the new rules. Think about it—of the 7,000 S&P companies, we were one of the top 9 over the last 10 years from a financial metrics standpoint. Our market cap had gone from $100 million to $9 billion. We'd been written about in every major business publication. Chico's had become the darling of the industry, and many of the key executives who got us there were leaving. Why? Because we knew that the consequences of not following the new rules would be the total breakdown of the effort.

Little more needs to be said about the importance of protocols to great teams.

Over the years, we have seen great teams develop a wide variety of protocols. At Redken Fifth Avenue, for example, senior vice president

General Manager Pat Parenty points to several protocols that were hammered out during his top team's alignment session and that guide everyone's behavior. "If a person has a conflict with someone else, they speak to that person first," explains Parenty. "If they can't resolve it, they talk to their manager." In addition, the team has adopted a 24-hour rule. "If a person has a disagreement or an issue with how someone else is handling things, within 24 hours they must agree to address it or drop it." Finally, a silence rule states that if a player does not speak up during a discussion, meeting, or informal interaction, it equates to a tacit endorsement of the decision or action.

All teams at Redken abide by similar protocols, and Parenty makes sure that they also possess the skills needed to resolve conflicts within this framework. For over a decade, all executives and managers at Redken USA have participated in conflict-resolution workshops. Since the company's move to a high-performance, horizontal model, it has boasted double-digit sales and profit growth—within an industry that has been expanding at an average rate of only 2%. Parenty believes that there is a cause-effect relationship. "We do not miss opportunities due to inaction or warring factions, and we make better, quicker decisions because we have these rules in place."

Parenty's latter comment brings us to the second area in which protocols are critical—decision making.

On great teams, the leader is no longer Mr. or Ms. Decision Maker. Much of the action shifts to subteams, where the decisions tend to be made by consensus or consultatively. Leader-centered decision making enjoys one paramount advantage. The decision process is clear: It's the leader, stupid! But as leaders migrate away from the leader-centered model, there is a potential for great confusion, which is why it is crucial for teams to develop and agree upon protocols for decision making. For example, how will important decisions be made—unilaterally, collaboratively, or by consensus? Who will be consulted for information? For opinions? Who will make the final decision? And who will execute it?

An important caveat about protocols: They are not created by the leader and imposed on the players as a fait accompli. The players and the leader, together, hammer out the new protocols. Here, commitment is key to compliance.

TEAM PROTOCOLS AT CHICO'S

Protocols are agreed-upon ways of working within the team in areas such as conflict resolution, decision making, meetings, and the expectations of team members and the team leader. Here are 10 protocols that have been used by Chico's FAS to create great teams:

1. Be candid and straightforward.
2. Be receptive to others' viewpoints.
3. Be accountable for *your* results and behavior.
4. Hold others accountable for *their* results and behavior.
5. Let go of "stories."
6. Resolve it or let it go.
7. Do not triangulate.
8. Do not accuse in absentia.
9. Depersonalize—feedback is a business, not a personal, issue.
10. Structure decision making.

Aligning Business/Interpersonal Relationships How easily a team reaches agreement in the four areas we have just discussed—strategy, goals, roles, and protocols—depends in large part on the relationships among its members—the fifth key element of alignment.

Dysfunctional relationships—not fuzzy strategy, shifting priorities, unclear roles and responsibilities, skill deficiencies, or lack of resources—are the single greatest impediment to a team seeking to elevate its level of play. And they are the most difficult to correct. Dysfunctional relationships frequently have their roots not in rational or even logical factors, but in psychological ones. Feelings, attitudes, and stories about oneself or one's colleagues reside within the individual. Aggression, passivity, abrasiveness, and other forms of acting out are often unconscious maladaptations — "reaction formations," in psychological terms—that are learned early on as ways to deal with trauma or stress. To the extent that these inner qualities show up as behaviors within a team—not keeping commitments, being uncommunicative, focusing on self-promotion rather than team interests, for example—then they can and should be addressed, with the aim being to modify behavior rather than correct underlying causes.

Given the profound performance impact of interpersonal relationships within a team setting, it is not unusual for us to begin the alignment here—especially when working with long-standing teams whose members have been relating to one another dysfunctionally for years.

One of the best ways to jump-start the process of changing the way players interact, while avoiding the "playing shrink" trap, is to conduct several exercises aimed at revealing the blind spots that players frequently have about themselves. We begin by asking players to reflect on their behavioral style and other traits or characteristics that may compromise their ability to establish healthy business relationships with colleagues.

We ask them to rate themselves in the following areas and to post their responses:

- Where on the continuum does your behavior generally fall when you are trying to get across your point of view? (nonassertive to assertive to aggressive)
- How do you play it with this team in terms of candor? (1 to 10 = closed to open)
- How receptive are you to feedback on your performance? (1 to 10 = not at all to totally)

Next, we ask the rest of the team to weigh in on each player's self-assessment, using the same scale. Each team member, including the leader, puts his or her scores and initials on every other person's easel sheet.

Each player then analyzes the others' feedback and tells the group:

- How his or her self-perception generally compared to that of others
- What he or she seems to be doing that is getting in the way of forging better relationships
- What he or she needs to do to raise the scores

When the analysis reveals significant disconnects, we ask each player to meet one on one with the colleague providing the feedback to discuss differences. It is crucial that the discussion be specific and behavior based. In other words, each person requesting a meeting should come prepared with the following information.

- My issue/opportunity with you is _____.
- The impact that this has on our business relationship is _____.
- In the future, I would like our interaction to look like _____.

The protocols for these one-on-one encounters—be direct and open, accept one another's feedback, attempt to reach a solution that will satisfy both parties, write down agreements and next steps in resolving the open issue—ensure that breast beating, psychoanalysis, and defensiveness are ruled out. After the alignment, back in the real world, the consultant and/or team leader will need to follow up with the players to assess progress and provide support and counsel.

Fairly easy and straightforward, right? Think again. This is one of the hardest exercises we ask a team to go through during an alignment. It is often a high-stakes, emotional moment. For many players who have avoided—often for years—a difficult discussion with a colleague, it is now confrontation time.

The senior pharmaceutical team whose prealignment responses we analyzed earlier was extremely apprehensive when we put it through this exercise. Recall that one member of this team—the head of Europe—was extremely aggressive in his interactions with others. The facilitator wisely began the self-assessments with his. As the executive posted his sheet, the anxiety level in the room became almost measurable. Was he going to deny it? Were they going to have to tell him the truth about himself? What should they say? How would he react? For the first time and to everyone's relief, he openly admitted that he was highly competitive—even combative—did not take feedback well, and made a habit of winning through intimidation.

His admission was an ice breaker. Feeling that they now had permission to agree with him, other players stepped forward to enumerate the difficulties his behavioral style was causing them and, one after another, they requested individual meetings with him. The head of R&D was next up to share his self-assessment. This time, the group had no trouble taking issue with his "pet projects for pet people" approach and telling him how uncomfortable they were speaking candidly to him.

It was a good beginning—but it was only that. During the alignment players wade only ankle deep into effective conflict management. They are introduced to a few of the skills—active listening, assertion, contracting[4]—and they spend time learning-by-doing on live issues; but two days is not enough time for mastery, which is why follow-up training and coaching are essential after the alignment.

How much progress is made during the alignment depends on a number of factors. Surely, the range of personality types on the team stands out as one such factor. When you think about it, organizations are almost random aggregations of people who find themselves required to work together closely. Ms. Dial Up and Mr. Dial Down must labor side by side to produce results, often under conditions of tremendous stress. Without a skilled team coach, ongoing skills training, and in many cases individual coaching, the flood gates are open for the domineering to dominate and for the passive-aggressive to sabotage team performance.

Cultural differences, especially on global teams, are another significant impediment to aligning relationships. Among these differences, language is one of the most difficult barriers to overcome. "The Idols of the Market-place"—errors that afflict us because of our choice and use of words—"are the most troublesome of all," Francis Bacon wrote way back in 1620 about the power of words to cause misunderstanding.[4] What would he say today, if he were present at a senior team meeting of the average global enterprise?

Paul Stoneham, who spent four years as managing director (chief executive) of Boots Healthcare International (BHI), where his team included Americans, Canadians, British, Indians, Italians, and Swedes, comments, "Even between British and American English, there are differences in the meanings of words, the subtleties, and the sense of humor." Stoneham believes that the team needs to go out of its way to make players feel comfortable as they try to express themselves in the group.

At BHI, the head of Europe was an Italian who spoke about people in a much more objective way than did the Brits on the team. His colleagues took exception to his seemingly detached analysis of financial performance and his proposal to reduce overhead. It lacked empathy, they felt. In fact, his colleagues were imposing their values and way of thinking and communicating on someone who was doing his best in a second language to present an objective case for supporting business goals. On an executive team, you should be able to have a robust discussion about how to take out overhead and then switch gears and talk about how to treat the people fairly, as opposed to having only the equitable discussion and not the business discussion. Without the rich vocabulary of English you can lose the subtleties, and they weren't listening generously as he tried to make his case.

Listening "generously," in Stoneham's phrase, means suspending initial judgment. Before members on a highly diverse team jump to conclusions about a colleague's capabilities or intentions, it is wise to test the source of whatever difficulty a non-English-speaking team member may be having. Is it an idiosyncrasy of language? A vagary of culture? Style?

Different cultures also have very different levels of comfort with conflict. It is well known that in the Far East people tend to be much less forthcoming during business meetings, especially with outside associates or higher-level executives in their own organization. And behavior that many Americans view as hospitality and friendliness can come across as too pushy or overly familiar to people who are used to building relationships over a long period of time.

Philosophical or religious differences also affect the way people prefer to deal with conflict. On one senior team I worked with recently, a fairly heated discussion arose during the alignment. I noticed that two of the players remained stone silent. When the argument subsided, I asked them if they had anything to add. One of them demurred, saying he was new to the team and did not feel qualified to offer an opinion. The other, a native of China, simply said, "No, I don't." When I asked if he ever became angry or frustrated, he replied, "Angry, of course not. Anger is not Buddhist; it is not Taoist." He did admit to sometimes being frustrated when conversations went on and on without resolution. How did he handle those emotions? "I feel them inside and keep them to myself," he confessed.

I pointed out that it was possible for him to express his frustration without violating his Buddhist or Taoism beliefs. In fact, he could add considerable value by letting the group know he was frustrated with endless discussion and suggesting the team move on either to making a decision or planning next steps for future resolution. I also suggested that he might help others who felt the same but did not have the courage to interject by prefacing his remarks with the question, "Is anyone besides me feeling frustrated by this discussion?"

This behavior required a significant change. My advice to the executive—seek individual coaching support to learn that it is possible to disagree without being disagreeable and that, when properly channeled, emotions that appear to be negative can have a positive effect.

Global and, of course, virtual teams are at another disadvantage when it comes to aligning interpersonal relationships. When players do not have an opportunity for face time, relationships are apt to become transactional rather than interactional in nature. Water-cooler conversations, informal lunchtime chatter, and small talk at breaks or before a meeting begins can be important socializing moments that help to foster common understanding. They enable team members to read one another's cues, both verbal and nonverbal, with greater precision than when there is little or no personal contact.

On teams whose communication does not include facial expressions, tone of voice, and body language, there is greater potential for misunderstanding. At VISTAKON®, a division of Johnson & Johnson Vision Care, Inc., the relationship between the company's Jacksonville, Florida-based R&D arm and its Irish manufacturing facility was strictly transactional. "There was no reason for us to interface or act as a team," explains Craig Walker, vice president of R&D, Product and Process Commercialization. "Products got transferred to Ireland after they were developed and initially manufactured here in Florida."

But when VISTAKON® adopted an ambitious new strategy to triple the number of new products brought to market each year, both R&D in Florida and plant operations in Ireland were forced to work closely together. Therein lay the problem. In the absence of interpersonal contact, each group developed stories about the other that stood in the way of effective teamwork. For example, the folks in Jacksonville believed that their Irish counterparts went about changing manufacturing equipment on a whim. Their Irish counterparts had a counterstory. "You folks in Jacksonville come up with lots of ideas. You never consult with us, never ask for input. You simply force them on us."

It was not until we brought both stories—and the storyholders—together in a room for an alignment session that the issues could be put on the table for discussion and resolution. The discussion often crackled with the point-counterpoint of accusations and misunderstandings. "What's the purpose of your group? Why do you exist?" the teams asked one another. Personal issues were raised. Old decisions were brought back from the dead for debate. Through it all, and given the discipline of the alignment process, both teams forged a deeper understanding of one another and of what it meant to shift gears to high-performance mode.

"Now," says Walker, "we have a mutual agreement as to what 'done' looks like. If there is disagreement we thrash it out. We created subteams to deal with some of the real pain points, especially around new regulatory requirements." They developed rules and standards and decided which would be followed. "Ireland was concerned about keeping costs down and delivering quality. R&D was interested in innovation and speed. We learned to balance short-term operational objectives with longer-term R&D objectives."

Aligning the business relationships between both groups has had significant performance payoffs. For example, during the recent launch of 1-Day Acuvue®, a new product in the contact lens category, the number of units produced per shift was ramped up to three times the previous levels, and on the "right the first time" metric, the need to go back and fix was at an all-time low.

To build strong, healthy business relationships on a team, we recommend that, no matter what mountains you have to move, you schedule at least one face-to-face meeting annually. Look for opportunities to piggyback team meetings with other corporate events, especially if budget is a constraint. If you can, allot extra time at your next meeting to getting to know one another. In working with newly formed teams, one of the exercises with which we frequently start alignments is designed to humanize players in one another's eyes.

Ask each player to take an easel sheet and tell, *in words and pictures*:

- Who is in their immediate family
- What their interests are outside work
- One to two career-defining moments that made them who they are today
- What they most value in themselves as a professional
- What strengths they bring to the team/what their fellow players can count on them for
- What they would most like to learn from others on the team
- The most important things they need from teammates in order to work together successfully

- What makes them crazy when they are working with others (i.e., hot buttons to avoid)
- Their best hope for this team's accomplishments

As each person talks about himself or herself, the room comes alive and the ice begins to melt. Even team members who have worked side by side for some time are often surprised to find out how little they knew about their colleagues and how much they have in common.

And about those pictures we ask players to draw, remember that there is nothing like a good, shared laugh to break the ice!

End Thought

The initial alignment process begins the journey to high performance. The fundamentals are in place for a team to navigate the Team Development Wheel. But in today's world time is more than money—it is also a competitive advantage. How can the journey to high performance be accelerated? That is the question we will address in the following chapter.

Notes

1. For the full story of Amado and his team's turnaround of IT at PMUSA, see Thomas Hoffman, "Good to Great," *ComputerWorld,* December 13, 2004.
2. Ibid.
3. For a full explanation of the skills needed by high-performing teams, see Appendix B.
4. Bacon, Francis. *Novum Organum*, translated by R. Ellis and James Spedding, George Routledge & Sons, Ltd., London. p. 71

5 | Accelerating to High Performance

Moving to Action

For me to play it completely authentically with everyone on this team, what story would I have to let go of?

This question is a deep-think one, the answer to which will determine whether individual players and the team will achieve greatness. Remember the senior pharmaceutical team whose data were presented in the previous chapter? The members of the team grappled long and hard with the question. They pointed to a number of stories:

- Conflict damages relationships.
- People will hold a grudge if I criticize/confront them.
- I'm too far away to interact with other regions on a regular basis.
- I can't trust my peers to do what they say they will.

- You don't understand how complex my area of responsibility is.
- People pigeonhole me as "the legal guy"; my opinion in other areas isn't valued.
- Commercial guys are focused on short-term sales goals; they don't have a long-term vision.
- I'm not given enough resources to do my job.
- Etc.

At this point in the alignment process, the players have significant insight into their personal strengths and weaknesses. They are aware of the behavioral changes they need to make and the skills they need to hone. They know exactly which key issues they need to resolve, with whom, and have come up with tangible agreements for moving forward. Team members have begun their transition to a high-performance team, with a clear idea of what they have to change. They have assumed responsibility for their transformation.

This is a critical juncture: the point at which the team starts to build on the momentum started during the alignment session. Continuing to move forward requires a concrete plan before the team disbands and players go back to the trenches.

An action plan developed by a high-performing team typically includes:

- *Follow-up*: Put in place a system for continuing the issue resolution started during the alignment. Who will follow up to ensure that the contracts made between players are honored? Does anyone else need to be involved in their discussions? What assistance might they need?
- *Organization barriers*: Have any impediments to higher performance been identified during the alignment? For example, a performance system that focuses on individual rather than team performance, a reporting structure that contributes to role confusion, overlapping responsibilities between departments that need to be clarified, and so on. Determine whose responsibility it is to ensure that these barriers are removed, who else needs to be involved, and how soon it can be done.
- *Skills*: Schedule formal skill-development workshops to address the skill gaps identified during the alignment.

- *Individual coaching*: Assign individual coaches to players who need extra help.
- *Team coaching*: Develop a plan for process coaching of the entire team in its interactions going forward.
- *Future business opportunities:* The team leader is to identify additional opportunities to begin following the high-performance model to address existing business issues.
- *Communication:* Agree on what the team will tell others in the organization about the session and what transpired during the two days.

Immediately following the alignment, the leader and players roll up their sleeves and get started. The objectives are clear: Get out the message—in writing and in person—to the next tier. Tackle the organizational issues that were identified. Schedule skill-development workshops and individual coaching sessions. Identify ongoing opportunities to use the concepts. Finally, one of the most important factors in accelerating performance—coaching for the team *as a team*—also needs to be arranged.

Accelerating Through Team Coaching

During every alignment, teams experience breakthrough moments, when they exhibit some of the attributes of a Stage 3 or Stage 4 team. The challenge is to go from breakthrough moments to consistent breakaway, Stage 4 performance. Accelerating through the stages requires close monitoring and team coaching in the real world.

Many organizations that we work with ask a senior executive—one who has "been there, done that"—to serve as the team coach, ensuring that the team remains true to its newly acquired horizontal way of operating. Others prefer to retain an outside consultant or to use a combination of internal and external resources.

Whether the team coach is employed by the organization or an outsider, he or she needs to be alert to these common red flags, which indicate that the team is veering off course:

- Team leaders who retreat to Grand Inquisitor or Solomon mode
- Too many "grey beard" issues that hang around forever
- Sidestepping delicate issues

- Protocols that fall by the wayside
- Failure to hold one another accountable for underperformance
- More "me" than "we" in the air

When inappropriate behaviors and interactions occur, the team coach must role-model the art of giving effective feedback—clear, behavior based, and depersonalized.

The CEO of an international consumer packaging company met recently in Europe with his company's divisional presidents to roll out a new global strategy. The initial response was enthusiastic, but one executive kept raising doubting Thomas-type questions. And, whenever this occurred, several of his fellow team members interjected with, "Good question" or "That's a good point." Listening with two ears, his colleagues heard only the words, which indicated that he was engaged in a legitimate search for information.

Listening with his "third ear," the team coach heard something different. All the questions were a veiled challenge to the CEO and his new strategy. Before the underground opposition could corrupt the discussion, the coach wisely stepped in to confront the situation. To the doubting Thomas he said, "I'm getting the message that you're not on board with the new strategy, but it seems as though, rather than stating your objections, you couch them by posing questions. Why not just say that you disagree?" Additionally, the coach asked of the other team members: "Why the collusion? Why are you pretending that he's asking the questions in good faith—to get information rather than to sabotage the rollout?"

The coach's questions cut through the subterfuge, and after honest discussion the colluders admitted that they had been willing to play along with the aggressive questioner in the hope that he would come around to the CEO's way of thinking. The doubting Thomas admitted that he had some private concerns, and he and the CEO agreed to discuss these "off line" if they continued to trouble him.

When people speak to one another, especially about charged issues, they often encode the message rather than state it directly. The coach must decode the message and feed it back to the speaker to ensure that the coach has it right. In the case of the doubting Thomas, the coach told both him and his colluders exactly what he had heard behind the words. He then communicated his understanding of the subtext of the messages. Once it became clear that the coach had gotten it, those involved acknowledged they had been playing a game. And only when both sides' messages had been decoded, fed back, and acknowledged was the group able to move forward and deal with the issues openly and effectively.

There arrives in just about every team coach's experience a time when he or she must "tell it like it is." To do otherwise is to risk becoming a colluder or coconspirator in dysfunctional behavior. This is a big-stakes moment in coaching, and walking the line between confronting and alienating others can be a perilous high-wire act. By accusing rather than reporting, blaming rather than explaining, coaches can easily lose the trust and respect of the people they have been hired to help.

Skilled team coaches are masters at giving feedback. First, they depersonalize feedback, presenting the facts without judging them.

Second, effective team coaches carefully formulate their comments. They work hard to avoid value judgments, both positive and negative. Whenever possible, they relate conclusions to observable behavior: "You say you are in agreement, but your tone of voice is angry and aggressive," or "You have told me you want to change your management style, but in the last meeting you held you cut off discussion several times."

Third, effective team coaches present the facts and then ask the individual or team to confirm or refute them, keeping the coach from being perceived as judgmental.

I recently worked with a group of executives who never seemed to reach closure, even after their initial alignment session. After each of their team meetings, the list of unresolved issues got longer and longer. They continually tabled resolution by requesting more information, raising more questions, and adding more complexity. I asked them, "Have any of you noticed that the group seems to keep passing the baton, and that nobody ever forces closure? Why do you think that is?"

My questions forced the team members to look at themselves the way an outsider would, and the pattern suddenly became clear to them. Once they realized how dysfunctional their behavior was, they were determined to uncover its cause. They admitted openly that their organization's culture discouraged people from taking responsibility for decision making; no one wanted to "own" decisions, so they simply kept postponing them. I did not tell them that. I described their behavior, as I saw it, and I asked them to draw their own conclusions. The moment of truth belonged to them, not me.

The underlying challenge for any team coach is to make team members 100% accountable for the outcomes of their interpersonal relationships.

A coach's charge—for which he or she, in turn, is 100% accountable—is to develop the abilities of others, by a combination of role-modeling and skills transfer, to interact as authentically as possible, in order to accelerate performance to the next level.

As Tom Coughlin, coach of the New York Giants, once put it, "Coaching is making players do what they don't want to do so that they can become what they want to become."[1] Amen.

How L'Oréal Paris Achieved High Performance

Since one example is often worth a thousand abstractions, here is a description of one team's journey toward greatness, including the road-blocks it faced and how it got through them.

David Waldock has been the senior vice president of sales for L'Oréal Paris for over 15 years. The division has been enjoying a long run of annual double-digit sales growth. Waldock's sales team is made up of vice presidents, including the national sales managers for each of the company's three categories—cosmetics, skin, and hair; the heads of sales operations and human resources; and team leaders for two major customers.

Waldock's team is a good example of what happens when the initial alignment session is not followed by leadership skills training and application of the new ideas under the watchful eye of a coach. Due to the lack of follow up, the team had to go through the alignment process more than once. Things didn't change for the better until the team made the full commitment and retained a coach.

At the time of its first alignment, the team was confused about strategy and goals. Players had been operating independently rather than interdependently, as they each focused on their functional responsibilities rather than their sales organization leadership role. Their tendency to personalize feedback had resulted in a high degree of tension. They were also quite pessimistic about their future, generally feeling that they were not going to be able to achieve long-term goals and become a team that could handle more adversity and more responsibility as sales growth became increasingly challenging.

Waldock believes that some of the team's problems stemmed from the fact that its members just did not have the leadership skills to play at a higher level. During the alignment, they grasped the concepts intellectually, but afterward there was no opportunity to internalize them. Two contributing factors: Since Waldock's team was the first in the organization to be aligned, there was no other team present to model the behaviors for them; and team members did not receive any further skills training or coaching after the initial alignment.

"In retrospect," Waldock reflects, "there were a lot of indicators that there was a deficiency of leadership skills. We were unable to participate in strategic discussions without immediately jumping into problem solving; we didn't have the ability to listen to another person's point of view without either trying to solve the problem or dismissing it; we never confronted one another; instead, everyone 'made nice' and pretended to agree on everything."

It was not until one of my colleagues began to coach the team on an ongoing basis that lasting breakthroughs occurred. He worked with them formally and informally on listening, assertion skills, and conflict-management skills. "Until then," says Waldock, "there had been a lack of true self-awareness on the team. We all had lots of blind spots. He held up the mirror to us, without brutalizing or damaging people, and made us see these clearly."

Waldock describes one of these blind spots:

We thought that we were working extremely well together, that we had a common approach and voice, and that the field sales organization was receiving good, consistent direction from us. When we took an honest look at ourselves, it became evident that that was not the case. One of the team members had an aggressive personality; another was passive-aggressive. Between them, a lot of factions had developed. On the surface everything seemed to be fine, but beneath the surface there were conflicts that had to be exposed, which the consultant did. He showed the team members how they were contributing to the dysfunction, if only by allowing it and not forcing a change.

The coach also helped them embrace the mindset needed to break through to high performance. "It took a lot of effort to get people to recognize that to be a high-performing team you have to do more than manage your function," recalls Waldock. "You have to be thinking about and participating in management of the sales organization as a whole."

In meetings, the coach remained focused on the team's *process*. When conflicts arose, he inserted himself and provided a running commentary on the dynamic that was being played out. "Once their dysfunctional interactions were pointed out to them," according to Waldock, "everyone wanted to improve. The willingness was there, or it would not have worked."

Waldock made another change that he believes was key to moving forward: What used to be called "Dave's staff meeting" became the "senior sales leadership team meeting." The agenda was no longer focused on the tactical elements of running the business: How are we doing this month? How is the launch proceeding? Will we be able to ship this big order? The team began tackling the strategic issues that were its unique responsibility: What issues are on the horizon that we need to prepare for? Where do our strengths lie? What skill gaps do we have that need to be filled? Do we have the bench strength we need? Tactical issues are now handled by the next level down, where they belong.

Team members began holding one another accountable for playing by the new rules. They asked one another to call them on their behavior if they were seen reverting to the old ways during a meeting. Even if the interaction was between Waldock and another player, the team was free to say, "Time out, you need to change your approach." They also stamped out triangulation by being rigorous about calling people on it before it had a chance to take root.

Like the model high-performance leader we described in Chapter 2, Waldock underwent a significant personal transformation. Like the rest of the team, during the alignments he "got it at the 100,000-foot view," but it was not until the team began dissecting his behavior and personal interactions that it really hit home. "Just because I was the titular head of the function didn't mean that I had the skills to be a member, let alone the leader, of a high-performing team," Waldock openly confesses. "I realized that I was lacking a number of skills that, as a senior manager, I should have had. Conflict-management skills were first on the list."

Waldock says that, for him, the hardest skill to master was holding others accountable for resolving their own conflicts. He also had to learn how to stop playing the "go-to guy." Other skills he worked hard to acquire: stepping aside and letting the team make its own decisions and chart its own course; calling players out when they revert to old behaviors; refusing to be drawn into triangulation and pointing out to the guilty party that it is not going to be tolerated; taking feedback on the chin—not challenging it, but acknowledging and acting on it; and, finally, refusing to permit the team to go back to dealing with operational issues during its meetings.

Sustaining High Performance

If the sales team at L'Oréal Paris had done some soul-searching after its first alignment, it would have realized that it had stalled, and it might have been able to get moving again. That is why we recommend that every team conduct informal and formal self-assessments on a regular basis.

Most high-performing teams that we know do a quick and informal reality check at the end of each regularly scheduled meeting, asking: How are we doing as a team? Are the ground rules we have established holding up? Are there any disconnects?

Some teams keep track of progress by asking a process observer to sit in on meetings and, at the end, comment on the team's behavior. Players can then move quickly to take corrective action.

Conduct Ongoing Reassessments

High-performing teams should go through a formal reassessment process every six months. After two years of investing in high-performance teamwork, Brian Camastral, Mars Inc.'s regional president, Latin America, initially blanched at the suggestion that his team go through another reevaluation session—especially since the team was performing well. "What in the world are we doing this for again?" he asked. But his reaction changed after the two-day reevaluation. "It really ramped up performance and made me realize that we should be doing this regularly, for the foreseeable future."

The reassessment process begins when each of the players answers the same questions that were posed prior to the alignment. Once again, responses are confidential, and only the consolidated data are shown to the leader and players. These data are then compared to the prealignment data to determine how much progress has been made, in which areas, and where additional coaching or training is needed.

The responses often uncover needs for additional skill building, especially in environments were there is high churn and complexity. According to Waldock, "Our management structure is very complex; we have three national sales managers who operate as a triumvirate. All share responsibility for issues that cut across the sales organization, such as standard policies and procedures, people development, succession planning, and the like. As you may imagine, this can give rise to a lot of conflict. Negotiating through these issues requires a great deal of skill, and we now make sure that everyone on the team can hold his or her own."

For Ken Bloom and his senior team at INTTRA, periodic reassessments are now a valuable mechanism for continuous improvement. "We no longer see the dramatic improvement in scores that we had at the beginning," says Bloom, "but nuance becomes more important and more telling. Maybe we don't go from a 4 to a 5, but we are more keenly aware of the definition of a 4. It reinforces the knowledge that this is an ongoing journey; you never get to 5 and wrap up the exercise. You are always redefining a 5, getting better at understanding it, even if you never get there."

Recalibration

High-performing teams are not perpetually high-performing entities. The real world is full of twists and turns—a new team leader, churn in team membership, restructuring, a strategic shift, an economic downturn, you name it. It is unrealistic to expect perpetual perfection from a team. When the leader or players feel that they are backsliding, it is time to recalibrate.

Chico's performance in the first years of the new millennium made it the Wall Street darling in its category. But by the time 2007 rolled around, the market was more competitive, and, in the face of gas-pump poverty, consumer spending had tightened. CEO Scott Edmonds realized that greater customer focus was needed. He and his top team moved to create three separate business units, each led by a brand president. This restructuring represented a radical change.

The disruption took its toll. Communication was not always clear. There was mounting anxiety among some top team members and those reporting to them about the implications of the changes on them and their operation. Resource allocation became a contentious issue, as did the assignment of top leadership positions. And conflict was headed underground, rather than being openly confronted.

Edmonds sensed that his team and those reporting to it were beginning to veer from the high-performance behavior they had so carefully nurtured. He moved quickly to bring us in to conduct a series of confidential, one-on-one interviews of members of both teams before probing further with an in-depth survey. The interviews and the survey confirmed Edmonds' suspicions: The two top teams were backsliding.

The Leader's Role in Recalibration

The leader of a high-performing team plays a pivotal role in a team's recalibration. His or her role goes well beyond spotting trouble and taking a barometric reading of team members. Edmonds was not content to let the team assessment become a vent-and-forget exercise. He called a two-day, off-site meeting of the senior team and its direct reports to confront the situation head on. In one especially revealing exercise, the group was divided into subteams and asked to write a headline on the current situation facing them. "No More B.S.; Clarify Roles or Move On," was one headline. "Too Busy for High-Performing Teams?" asked another.

Clearly, this was going to be a tough two days. The headline exercise was followed by Edmonds opening up the discussion to a no-holds-barred Q&A session in full group. In effect, he put himself in the hot seat to field questions and comments from the group: "How are resources going to be allocated to the three new business units? What's the timing of the restructuring? Who will be accountable for what?" Edmonds' answers were honest and forthright. Where decisions were yet to be made or were too sensitive to be discussed in full group, he said so.

Here is the point: You cannot move from breakdowns to breakthroughs without the team leader demonstrating openness to rigorous questioning and feedback. And when the leader is open, team members are apt to follow.

"Us" Accountability

Leadership aside, accountability is another prerequisite for bringing a star team back up to its previous level of performance. Dips in team performance are rarely the result of a single underperformer. In most cases, the enemy is "us." On high-performing teams, accountability goes well beyond the individual's recognition that he or she is part of the problem. It even goes beyond holding peers on the team accountable for performance. *"Us"* accountability includes holding the team leader accountable as well.

That is precisely what happened during Chico's off-site session. One segment of the two-day session was devoted to having each team member answer two questions and note his or her responses on an easel: What do you want a team member to do differently? What do you want that team member to continue doing? This was accountability time! For example, on the "Discontinue" list, the COO was told to "stop moving slowly on weak staff talent" in a particular business unit. Other requests made to the senior team included "Stop being negative" and "Share concerns about a decision with the person involved before sharing it with others." One-on-one discussion followed between the individual providing feedback and the one receiving it. The full-group discussion that followed was frank, tough, and focused on behavior and action.

Passion for Action

"Just do it." These are three powerful words. High-performing teams, especially those in recalibration mode, are relentlessly action oriented. They typically have a built-in issue-resolution process—identify issues, set priorities, assemble the fewest number of people from the team needed for resolution, set decision-making guidelines, and move quickly to resolution.

Chico's top team and the team that reported to it began the issue-resolution process just described. Once issues were identified and subteams created, those subteams were asked the following questions, in full group: In order to resolve this issue, what do you need from each of the individuals and functions you will have to interact with? What behaviors do they need to exhibit in order to help you ratchet up your performance? This process made "just do it" a full-team accountability.

Recalibration is difficult to achieve when team members find themselves unable to break away from old patterns and limitations. This is the time for coaching and training in a variety of skills, such as conflict management, influencing, and leadership.

Recalibrating a sluggish high-performing team is rarely a mission impossible. Team members who were once at the top of their game need to be reminded of the fundamentals in order to return to the previous level of play.

End Thought

"The persona of a team comes through most sharply in how the team operates day in and day out." Craig Williams, director of human resources for Johnson & Johnson Vision Care, has a point. How does a high-performing team solve problems, make decisions, plan, conduct meetings, and communicate with colleagues on the team and with the wider organization? Once a team is fully aligned and properly coached, what is its "persona?"

These are the questions we will address in the next three chapters, as we look at how great teams make decisions, manage meetings, and communicate.

Note

1. *The New York Times,* February 24, 2007, p. B12.

6 | How Great Teams Make Decisions

By their deeds—and their decisions—ye shall know them. Surely, a team's track record in making decisions is one foolproof indicator of whether or not it is operating at the top of its game.

Decision making in teams is a social act. Even when it is a solo performance by an individual team member, chances are a decision has an impact on other team players. How do great teams structure the social space that a team operates in to increase the probability of decision-making success? This is the first question that we explore in this chapter.

While decision making offers a useful vantage point for assessing how great teams conduct business, it is not the only one. Much can be learned by observing how great teams manage meetings and how they communicate between and among one another.

This chapter and the two that follow are rigorously "how to," as we search for answers to two fairly provocative questions: Is there a set of high-performing decision-making, meeting-management, and communication behaviors? If so, what can we learn about these behaviors that will enable us to take another step toward cracking the code for standout performance?

Decision Making in Action

- **After the merger of Pfizer's and Warner-Lambert's consumer healthcare businesses, Craig Williams represented HR on the merged company's North American Leadership Team.** With Williams as liaison, the team began a significant alignment process, which took the team from Stage 1 to Stage 4 in 1½ years.

   Prior to the alignment, the team's decision-making approach was what you would expect from Stage 1 players. Says Williams, "At the beginning, the leader would get the team together, and they would have a discussion that was dominated by one or two people. Most of the players didn't voice their opinion. Then, the leader would make the decision and there would be compliance. If any of the players disagreed with the choice, they went underground, triangulating and creating alliances of malcontents."

   What happened when the same team of players upped their performance to Stage 4? According to Williams, "Issues were brought to the table and discussed openly. Everyone had an opportunity to speak. The entire team decided, together, what mode was going to be used to make each decision. If team members had any problems with the results, they raised their concerns in the meeting room. That became very rare, however, and most of the time everyone supported the decisions after leaving the room."

- **As chief learning officer for Mars Incorporated, Jon Shepherd is a member of a global HR team that meets infrequently.** Team meetings tend to coincide with Mars's worldwide management meetings, which the leader of the HR team must also attend, making him unable to meet with his own team. Prior to becoming a great team, in the leader's absence weeks would pass while the team waited for him to evaluate a decision and give it the thumbs up or down. Now the global HR team has turned decision delay into fast action. What has changed, among other things, are the new decision-making protocols that govern the team, which no longer require the leader to be present every time a decision is made. Shepherd points to a major decision—how to fill four vacancies for regional learning and development directors—that was raised by him, discussed by his subteam of three or four, and resolved in a few days instead of the weeks it would have taken under the old way of operating.

- **Novartis Oncology's executive team had a weakness for full-group discussion.** An issue—say, a new marketing thrust—would surface and the entire team would weigh in before sending it up to CEO David Epstein, who made the final call. This time-consuming process is no longer in practice. Now that it operates as a high-performing team, only those team members who have the most content knowledge are involved in the information-gathering and analysis phases of decision making. When the company's breast cancer drug, Femara, was second to market for a specified indication, the team needed to decide how to position the drug worldwide. Should they take a broad approach, going after multiple segments of breast cancer patients, or should they focus on those patients who were likely to receive the greatest benefits? A subteam—made up of the global head of Marketing, the European head of Marketing, the North American SVP, medical people in two countries where the drug was going to be launched, and the Femara brand leader—was charged with assessing these and other alternatives and making a recommendation to the full team. The recommendation was presented, discussed by the full group, and approved, saving a tremendous amount of time and unnecessary input. For the record, the team chose to adopt a *wedge* strategy, targeting the product to women whose breast cancer was most likely to recur. Within the first year, market share rose substantially.

- **During the alignment of L'Oréal USA's HR function, protocols were established for addressing the tougher issues more directly in order to ensure that all points of view were heard, in real time.** The team agreed that unanimity was not required for decision making, but that once a decision was made it would be supported by all. One example of turning this new alignment into action was the talent-review process, which was implemented in a consistent way across all divisions; and, despite differing points of views on the best alternative, all team members aligned behind the agreed-upon process. Greenberg says, "This model of debate and consensus is the key to how our team operates. I count on them to express their views, and we count on each other to support the final decisions."

■ **At about the same time that the senior team of Pfizer's international consumer healthcare business began to work on taking its performance to a higher level, the company decided it needed to be more innovative.** The problem: The senior team could not agree on what "innovation" meant, never mind how to drive it through the organization. The full team met for a four-hour skull session to define innovation and develop a plan to operationalize it. But progress was slow, so, like any great team, this one decided it was to time to assign the issue to a subteam of four people, with clearly defined objectives, deliverables, time lines, and a process for decision making. The subteam's charter: Arrive at a common definition of innovation; then, identify what, specifically, in the company's culture needed to change so that commercially smart innovations—new ways of creating competitive advantage—could be delivered on an ongoing basis.

Working as a tightly focused, fully engaged unit, the subteam cut quickly through the generalities. The end result was a clear, integrated road map for driving the change that resonated with the entire team. Says Rick Rizzo, then-president of the international business unit, "The big aha was realizing, for the first time, that we needed to be working not only on projects that were aligned with strategic priorities, but also on initiatives that would help shift the culture: specific training initiatives, specific communications initiatives, specific efforts focused on supporting individual leaders and how they drive cultural change in their area of responsibility."

Consistently great decisions do not happen by chance. Great teams follow a decision-making process. Before we describe in detail the typical decision-making process of great business teams, keep in mind three overarching points that help to explain why great teams are well primed for decision making.

First, great teams are strategically focused. Recall that high-performing teams are guided by a clear business strategy, which forms the basis of team alignment. Strategy establishes an organization's future competitive advantage and guides the allocation of resources. But it also does something else. When high-performance leaders establish where the business is going, team members can focus on *how to get there.* The high-performance leader puts operational, day-to-day decision making—the *how to get there*—largely into the hands of the team, which is in keeping with the high-performing, distributive approach discussed in Chapter 2.

Second, the high-performing model counteracts the social pressure on group members to conform to the majority view—helping it overcome a significant disadvantage, especially when a team faces important decisions.

In the 1950s, social psychologist Solomon Asch conducted a number of experiments that showed how susceptible individuals are to "group think." In one series of experiments, Asch assembled a group of seven people, all of whom were his confederates. An eighth subject—a stranger who was unaware of the status of the seven others—was added to the group. All eight were shown a pair of cards.

In each case, the card on the left contained one vertical line, and the card on the right three lines of varying length. Each of the eight participants was asked, one at a time, to choose the line on the right card that was the same length as that on the left card. Unbeknownst to the subjects, the seven confederates of Asch had been instructed to give the wrong answers. About one-third of the subjects went along with the clearly erroneous majority, in spite of what their own eyes told them. For them, seeing was not believing.

Why did the subjects conform so readily? When they were interviewed afterwards, most said that they had gone along with the group for fear of being ridiculed or considered "peculiar."[1]

Asch's and later experiments[2] demonstrate clearly that in any group—including business teams—there is a strong tendency to conform to the majority opinion for those same reasons. High-performing teams counter this tendency in a number of ways. First, by insisting on "mini board of directors" and "go there" attitudes. Second, by emphasizing personal accountability. Third, by demanding—and establishing protocols for—healthy confrontation and authenticity in business relationships. Fourth, by transferring much of the responsibility for decision making to subteams.

The third point about great decision-making teams: The high-performance decision-making model is built for speed, quality, maximum accountability, and engagement. Decision discussion begins with the team, through a process of issue identification, clarification, and priority setting. Further discussion lays out the plan of attack: Is this a decision for the full group to make or can it be decided by a subteam? If a smaller group is appropriate, what is the smallest number of people essential to arrive at either a decision or at least a recommendation? Once selected, ground rules and timelines are then established to bring the issue to a decision or a recommendation. Again, this distributive approach reduces decision clog, taps the brain power of team members, and puts decision making in the hands of those with the best available—and easiest access to—information.

Even today, a surprising number of executives continue to believe that decision making is principally a matter of gut feel and intuition. Truly, having an acute sixth sense is a great asset for a decision maker. But proceeding "by ear" is as reliable as rolling dice—it is essentially a gamble. Besides, how can you train others who are less well endowed?

What distinguishes great teams is their process, or structure, for decision making. That process channels information, experience, and gut feel, thereby increasing the probability of success. Having a process does more than guide the search for information related to objectives, alternatives, and risks—the foundational elements of every good decision; it also helps remove the emotional sting related to decision making. As Gerard Kells, vice president, HR, Operations and Technology for Johnson & Johnson, observes, "If you have clarity about how things are going to be done, and there's nothing hidden about how decisions are going to be made, it removes the potential for hard feelings on a personal level. It sounds so incredibly simple, but it's elegant in its simplicity."

Then there is the matter of implementation. The troublesome deciding–doing divide is not an issue on high-performing teams. Speaking from his experience on a great team, Kells sees the connection between having a clear process for channeling input and the ability to implement. "People have to know that there's a process and that it includes input. If I'm a member of a management team, and I come to my staff and say, 'Well, look, here's this decision that got made and I don't believe in it, and frankly, no one even consulted me,' I'll get a very different result than if I come back to my staff and say, 'Look, after a long debate and discussion, this is the decision that we made and I stand by it.'"

Let us look at the process that great teams follow when making decisions.

How a Great Team Makes Decisions

While we are not recommending that every team rigidly follow the same decision-making process and protocols, there are certain steps that aligned teams typically take to ensure that their decisions are as speedy and effective as possible.

- **Identify the decisions that need to be made.**

Whether intact or time limited, crossfunctional or intrafunctional, every team is responsible for an array of decisions. The full team begins by developing a laundry list of these. The question here is not *who* will make which decisions? Rather, the question is *which* key decisions will the team be making? How can these decisions be categorized: those related to strategy, project deliverables, personnel, budgeting, scheduling, and so on? And what are the priorities?

- **Identify decision subteams.**

For each decision or category of decisions that the team identifies, great teams form a subteam that, in effect, becomes a steering committee responsible for either making the decision or presenting a recommendation to the full team. The guiding principle: Identify the *smallest number* of people whose point of view adds value. In some cases, the leader will be a subteam of one who makes the decision unilaterally. Most of the time, however, the subteam will be made up of two or three people.

- **Assign accountability.**

Every subteam needs a point person: one individual who is responsible for driving closure. The chosen individual should be process focused, able to depersonalize, and someone who sees the big picture. Here, the most important selection criterion is not the player's job title or content knowledge but *process capability and the ability to get things done.*

Great team leaders avoid the overextended-leader syndrome, which arises when the leader serves as the point person on too many subteams. It comes dangerously close to the old hierarchical model.

- **Set objectives and timelines**.

Not every subteam is a decision-*making* body; frequently, a subteam gathers the facts, conducts a preliminary analysis, and brings a recommendation to the full team. It is important to clarify how much authority the subteam is being given and to gain agreement on when the subteam will present its conclusions to the full group.

- **Select the decision-making mode.**

Decisions often become entangled because it is not clear how, precisely, they will be made. There are three basic decision modes:

  - *unilateral*—made by one person with no input from others, and most appropriate for technically/functionally oriented decisions
  - *consultative*—made by an individual player or the leader after getting input from others
  - *consensus*—everyone on the team has input and everyone must agree to live with the outcome, even if it was not their first choice

Although high-performing teams make most of their decisions consultatively, no one mode is necessarily superior to another. In many cases, it matters less which mode is chosen for which decision—what is important is that everyone agrees on and adheres to the selected mode.

- **Identify information sources.**

If the decision or recommendation is to be made consultatively, one additional step remains to be carried out before the subteam goes off to do its work: Identify those individuals, on the team and outside it, who should be tapped for information and insight.

- **Determine the shelf life of the decision.**

Few decisions are forever. On great teams, every decision comes with walking papers. Assumptions, market conditions, technology, government regulations, and Murphy's Law make change inevitable. Part of the decision process of great teams involves setting a postdecision review date for assessing whether it is best to hold fast, make modifications, or overturn the original decision.

The Challenges

Like many other new high-performance behaviors—such as climbing the Accountability Ladder, delivering honest feedback, or changing personal behavior—distributive decision making runs counter to the standard practice within hierarchical environments. Here are a few common challenges that teams we have worked with have faced and overcome.

Which Decision Mode, When?

One of the most difficult challenges a team faces is deciding which mode to use for which decisions. As we have already noted, choosing the right decision mode can be less important than ensuring that the entire team agrees with the choice. But there are a few caveats to keep in mind.

First, be sure that everyone understands what consensus decision making implies. Unlike the requirement for juries in a capital-murder trial, it does not mean that unanimous consent must be given before an alternative is selected. This sets up an unrealistic expectation and inevitably leads to disappointment, as Linda Scard-Buitenhek, former vice president, cleansing platform, skin care, Johnson & Johnson's Consumer Products, discovered. "Teams that don't clearly define consensus beforehand are expecting that there will be total agreement on everything: lots of handholding, cooperation, feeling good. Not so. They need to know that there will be even more emphasis on working individually, on individuals taking the ball and running with it."

In a high-performance environment, *consensus means being able to live with the choice favored by the majority of the group.* Mark Stevenson, a member of Applied Biosystems' top team, never understood what that meant until Cathy Burzik introduced the team to the high-performance model. "The biggest change in my behavior," he reflects, "was my willingness, outside the team, to support the team's decisions. In the past, I hadn't always agreed with the team's decisions, and I was tempted to tell others that. But on a high-performing team, there are no hands from the grave. You agree to live with the decision and support it afterwards, even if you haven't gotten your way."

Caveat number two: Make sure that unilateral decisions—especially those made by the leader—do not predominate. Indeed, there are times when someone has to make the final call, and it is only natural that the leader be the one to cast the deciding vote, especially when the team reaches an impasse. However, as Larry Allgaier—global CEO of Novartis OTC—says, "final-call" decisions on the part of the leader should never be made without plenty of input: "If you walked into one of our team meetings during a heated discussion you wouldn't know who the leader was. I invite contentious debate; I don't try to control it. It's the best way to get good solutions. But if, at the end, there's a tough call to be made, they look to me to make it. They want me to show that on some level there is still a 'boss' with whom the buck stops. In these cases, I need to role-model decisiveness."

Helen McCluskey, president, Warnaco Intimate Apparel and Swimwear Group, believes that a great leader is a "balance of contradictions: someone who is a very good collaborator, but very decisive when needed." To observe her at a meeting is to witness the loose-tight style of high-performance decision making in action. When she was group president of Intimate Apparel, Warnaco, McCluskey's team was preparing for an important meeting with a major department store. She and her VPs of marketing, merchandising, sales, and so on were brainstorming about brand positioning and differentiation. After some time, she realized that they were going around in circles—spinning their wheels and going nowhere, with a very important meeting coming up and a deadline to meet. She said, "We have three segments of business here, we design and develop against those three segments. Figure out how we stack up against the market. That is our point of difference, that's how we add value to our customer, and that's how we will drive this business."

What determines the tipping point, when she moves from consultative to unilateral mode? "It's reached," McCluskey says, "when the team is not making any progress and time is against a long exploration. Someone has to come in and make a decision to keep things moving."

Who Should Be Involved?

After Rick Rizzo and his current team initially set protocols for determining who should be involved in which type of decision, they discovered that reality sometimes dictates otherwise. For example, on more than one occasion a subteam felt that more debate or information on a particular issue was needed, but this was difficult to accomplish, given the relatively large number of people on the subteam. It then shifted responsibility to a smaller number of people, making clear what deliverables were expected and who should receive them: Was the subteam asking the smaller group to go and make the decision or to come back with a recommendation? Was the smaller group expected to report back to the subteam or the full team? What was the time frame? Says Rizzo, "We wouldn't allow ourselves to end the discussion with soft, fuzzy objectives. We tried to really nail down the details, and if we didn't, someone would say, 'That's not clear. We can't leave it like that' or, 'Why are we asking six people to be on the team, when two should be enough?'"

High-performing leaders are astute at balancing the often-conflicting needs of decision-making efficiency and engagement. Larry Allgaier tends to give the latter added weight, but not without establishing clear ground rules. "If a decision impacts only Mexico," he says, "I could tell the head of China that he isn't needed on the subteam. But maybe one day I'll have to pull resources from China to drive business in Mexico, so I'd like him to be familiar with the big picture as well as with his region." Allgaier says that in cases where he errs on the side of including more players on a subteam than are absolutely necessary, their role is clear: They are there for informational purposes, not to make the final decision.

How Do You Let Go?

One executive who has held top leadership positions in a number of major companies knows how tough it is for many leaders to accept new decision-making protocols. "You have to fight your gut desire and normal inclination to make decisions," he observes. "You got your job because you are a great decision maker, someone who is able to get things done. But that's no longer your primary role."

He is right. Great leaders of great teams are often cast not only as decision *makers*, but also as decision *mentors*. They are responsible for ensuring that the organization's decision-making machine is whirring along: The right issues are being addressed; the right people are being deployed; decisions are being made in a timely fashion; and they are seamlessly communicated and implemented. They learn to multiply good decisions, not just make them.

Great leaders also refuse to be drawn into the content trap. When an individual player or subteam comes back to them with a recommendation, they test the *process* that was used, not the information, unless there is a critical need to do so. Chico's Chuck Nesbit explains, "When someone comes to me and says, 'I've decided to put in a process for the new accounting system. I want to use this software package,' it's not for me to say, 'I've had bad luck with that package; I've had better luck with this one, so use it.' As leader, my job is to make sure the person has done the due diligence, that his or her logic is correct, that he or she is aware of the risks. If the person has done all that, and has agreed to be accountable for making it work, it's not my place to override the decision. I have hired this person to deliver, and if I don't have confidence in the individual I need to look for a replacement, not make the decision myself."

Letting go is not only a challenge for high-performing leaders. It is also challenging for players, who must overcome the tendency to believe that their personal input is essential to the success of a decision or their involvement is necessary to ensure that their functional or personal needs are properly represented. Rick Rizzo likens the mind shift to becoming comfortable with "the idea of jumping off the ledge together—taking a leap of faith and believing they will land on their feet." He adds: "The more we did this and 'nobody died,' the more we began to realize that we were working with some very bright people who weren't operating in a parochial way, but were working in the spirit of what's right for the entire region. The more people saw that, the more they trusted the process."

If trusting peers on your team is tough, try transferring decision-making responsibility to the next tier. As Joe Pieroni recounts, "Our whole senior team, including myself, had to let go of the idea that we needed to be involved in every decision." Pieroni describes the process his team used to get past this barrier. During their alignment, it became apparent that decisions were not being made at the correct level: His direct reports were diving down into the issues, barely making it back up for air. When it came time to set decision-making protocols, the team identified about 15 decisions that had to be made. For example: What should be the configuration of our newly expanded field sales force? How many sales forces should we have? How many people should be in each? Which products should be allocated to each? What will be the timing? For each, they attempted to answer the questions: Who will lead the decision-making team? Who will be on the team? What do we want them to do? Every time someone suggested that one of them lead a team, the rest stopped and asked, why should we be involved in the decision-making process? In most cases, they realized that they did not have to be; they just needed to be informed.

But, Pieroni cautions about distributive power: "You can't just back away and let people think you are abdicating decision-making authority. They have to know that you are pushing it down and why."

Dealing with Bad Decisions

Even great teams make their share of mistakes. In an interview published by Harvard Business School's *Working Knowledge*,[3] Professor Amy Edmondson found that well-led teams *seem* to make more mistakes than average teams. The reason: They report and discuss more errors—then learn from them. It is not a far-fetched point, given the openness of great teams. Professor Edmondson underscores the self-correcting nature of high-performing teams. An equally distinctive feature is their willingness to step up and accept accountability for a bad decision. The former president of a global consumer products company recalls one dark moment after a major relaunch of a skin care brand. After making what they thought was an excellent decision, his team learned that it had based its choice on fundamentally flawed market research. As a result, the relaunch fell short of expectations. "In the past," says the executive, "individuals would have been blamed: the region, the marketing team, the marketing director, the agency, etc." In the new, high-performance world, the president himself took responsibility. "I wanted to model the mindset that, 'We are all in this together,' he explains, as opposed to the old attitude that 'someone screwed up.' We made the decision together, we all shared culpability, and, as team leader, it was ultimately my responsibility."

You Know It's Working When . . .

Frank Maione, former vice president of sales for Pfizer's Consumer Division, used to lead most of his team's meetings. Then, in keeping with the high-performance model, he started handing this responsibility off to other players.

Eventually, whenever Maione's commitments conflicted with a team meeting, the team met without him—and did not seem to miss a beat.

Maione realized that his team was up to the decision-making task by the way it handled a number of potentially contentious issues. In one case, a team member was about to make a poorly considered decision that raised the eyebrows of others on the team: He had decided, unilaterally, to promote someone. Acting as business owners who were unafraid to cross territorial lines, the team members let their colleague know that they did not agree with his choice and asked him to consider the implications of going ahead. The frank discussion gave this individual a broader perspective, and with eyes wide open he ultimately made a much better decision.

Maione tells us that this happened several other times after he began investing his team with greater decision-making responsibility, and he never heard about it until after the fact. High performance is working as advertised.

TEAMS AND DECISIONS: OVERCOMING THE CHALLENGES

In our observations of leaders and teams who have gone through the process of distributing decision-making authority, we have identified a number of traps into which teams typically fall, along with tips to counteract them:

Deferring to the Leader

Team members accustomed to working in a hierarchical organization will tend to defer to the leader. Team leaders must refuse to play Solomon or Monkey in the Middle. Unless they are part of a subteam, they need to be judicious about offering their opinion to that team. And they need to hold subteams accountable for making the decisions assigned to them.

The More, the Merrier

When assigning members to subteams, remember that *value added* is the key criterion. Be sure that everyone who is appointed will contribute to the decision-making process. The price of admission should be proficiency, not position.

Clueless about Closure

Because a person has technical knowledge or occupies a certain position on the organization chart does not mean that he or she should be the point person for a decision. Driving a decision to closure requires influencing others and keeping them in process; these are leadership, not technical skills. If a selected point person does not have the full array of necessary skills, arrange for coaching right away or think about a replacement.

Forced Unanimity

Everyone on the team needs to understand the definition of *consensus*: All team members do not have to agree with a decision, but they must be able to live with its outcome. Do not permit a subteam to try to lobby other players; do make sure that everyone on the team makes a public commitment to abide by the decision once it is made. Do not permit "hands from the grave," or second-guessing the subteams.

Notes

1. http://www.age-of-the-sage.org/psychology/social/asch_confor mity.html
2. A more recent study in this area, which underscored the importance of culture as a factor in conformity, is: Nibler, R. & Harris, K.L. (1994). "A Comparison of Group Consensus Decision Making: Chinese and American Cultures," in *Research and Practice in Human Resource Management,* 2(1), 35–45.
3. Gilbert, Sarah Jane. "Are Great Teams Less Productive?" Harvard Business School *Working Knowledge,* April 23, 2007.

7 | How Great Teams Manage Meetings

The Trouble with Meetings

Checking e-mail. Text messaging. Balancing the checkbook. Making a to-do list for the weekend. Surreptitiously leafing through a mail-order catalogue or doing a crossword puzzle. These are just a few of the activities that captive team members engage in during the long, dull meetings they are forced to attend. In most offices, just saying the word "meeting" is likely to provoke a chorus of groans. An article in *OfficeSolutions*[1] magazine estimates that typical managers spend nearly 40% of their work hours in meetings and cites a survey of business leaders that revealed the following:

- 33% of the time spent in meetings is unproductive.
- 75% of respondents said that it is "almost essential" to have an agenda; yet, they use it only 50% of the time.
- Only 64% of meetings achieve their desired outcome.

If you were to take a similar survey of your organization's teams, how do you think their answers would compare? Would most say their meetings were worth attending? Or would they describe them the way Mars Inc.'s president, Paul Michaels, talks about his global team's meetings in the prehigh-performance world:

> We wasted a lot of time in meetings. There was no rationale to the agenda, so we never dealt with the actual issues. We dealt with a lot of small issues, but not with the big ones or the right ones. There were a lot of moose heads in the room that we didn't talk about. For example, a lot of people weren't performing as they should, but no one held them accountable. People either didn't say anything or quickly became disengaged. Our global meetings were viewed as energy draining and unproductive. People couldn't wait to get back to their region.

Like so much else about his team, says Michaels, meetings are vastly different in the new, high-performance culture. No longer drawn-out, dreaded events, they are now swift-moving, productive sessions in which key issues are put on the table. If issues are not resolved then and there, the team develops a detailed plan for resolution and reviews it the next time they convene. As a result, the team, which Michaels says used to operate at 35 to 40% capacity, now works at peak efficiency.

How does a team like Michaels' transform its meetings from dull to dynamic?

Start with Protocols

We have spent a good deal of time talking about protocols: for conflict resolution, for decision making, for interpersonal behavior. There is another area in which having ground rules, or protocols, is key to moving from Stage 1 to Stage 4 behavior. You guessed it: meetings.

We all know from personal experience how quickly a meeting can spin out of control. A weak leader; an unruly participant; a room that is too hot or too cold; cell-phoneitis; the turnstile effect, with team members moving in and out of the room—any one of these factors can cause a meeting to derail. The great teams we know have eliminated these and numerous other barriers to effective meetings by setting up specific, hard-and-fast rules either during their alignment or soon thereafter.

When they set out to create new protocols for meetings, teams are invariably amazed at how much of their meeting behavior has been determined by "the cake of custom"—"We've always done it this way"—and how little of it is based on the need to continually ramp up meeting effectiveness. Taking a zero-based budgeting approach to how you conduct meetings is usually an eye opener. There are no right answers to meeting management; each team needs to carefully weigh its individual needs to come up with the right formula for success.

With that said, great business teams set basic protocols for the following aspects of meetings:

How Often Will the Team Meet and How Long Will Meetings Last?

Newly formed or newly aligned teams frequently feel the need for more meetings of longer duration. As they become more familiar with one another and the high-performance model, face-to-face, full-group meeting time shrinks.

For example, we recently attended a regularly scheduled meeting of Ken Bloom's senior team at INTTRA, which had been working in high-performance mode for the previous 12 months. The agenda, circulated in advance, called for no less than eight segments, each carefully laid out with subpoints; point person; and length of time for discussion, status, and actions.

Within each of the segments, the point person reported on the status of work on key business issues and, where necessary, solicited ideas and assistance from the group to continue their resolution. For instance, the seventh presenter was the VP of HR. In the 15 minutes allotted to her, she planned to cover the following—and she did:

Topic
7. Human Resources Update
7.1 Hiring Status (Open Requisition Report)—Issues
7.2 Head Count & Healthcare Cost—Budget Impact
7.3 IPMS 2007 Goal Roll-Out—Dept Heads Report In
7.4 Transition Status

In just 3½ hours, INTTRA's senior team discussed each issue—from information technology to product management to ocean schedules. They questioned each presenter, made suggestions, and pointed out potential problems and opportunities. The meeting was an impressive testament to the speed and effectiveness that an aligned team works at to conduct its business.

Protocols for issue resolution are one of the most effective ways to shorten meeting time. Remember how Rick Rizzo, former international president of Pfizer's Consumer Healthcare business, and his entire team spent four hours trying to define and operationalize *innovation*? It was not until it began handing off such thorny issues to subteams that the team's marathon meetings finally ended.

Where Will the Team Meet?

This is not usually a major issue for teams whose members are located within commuting distance of one another. Here, the most attention needs to be paid to "hygienic" factors, such as meeting room atmospherics, layout, and even the thermostat. But do not underestimate the impact of hygiene on performance. We worked with the CEO of a prestigious West Coast architectural firm. Here is his field report: "When I joined the company, there were conference rooms with huge tables, where everyone worked individually, with a red pencil, poring over a set of blueprints. 'Where's the white board?' I asked. 'How do I get to work in front of the team; share my ideas by making them visible; brainstorm, collaborate, and manage projects in an integrated way?'" The architectural environment was not conducive to working as a high-performing team.

There is a lot more to the "where" when you are dealing with a team whose members are not located near each other. We have mentioned it before, but it is worth reiterating: Global teams face special challenges when it comes to meetings, and creativity is a must if the far-flung members are to become at-a-distance great teams. It is imperative that the team meet face-to-face as often as possible. Create the opportunity to do so by piggybacking team meetings onto other corporate functions. Think about taking the show on the road by occasionally meeting in regional offices. Doing so gives personnel in remote locations a chance to meet the members of the global team, and it gives regional team members a chance to showcase their operations.

In an effort to make the most of their limited face-to-face time, Rizzo's global team began planning evening social events in conjunction with meetings. "We made it mandatory that everyone go to dinner together on the first night instead of allowing people to opt out," explains Rizzo. "The more time we spent together, the more interpersonal connectivity we developed. When we got back to business, members' ability to trust one another had increased, as had their desire to engage with one another."

When they cannot be in one location, patching remote members in by phone or videoconference still provides valuable interaction—provided you keep in mind time zones, non-U.S. holidays, and local religious observances when scheduling. Think globally, act globally!

Who Will Lead Meetings?

Craig Williams, now director of human resources for Johnson & Johnson Vision Care, likens one team he served on, when it was in Stage 1, to "the leader holding court." Explains Williams, "He went through the agenda items one by one, asking for discussion. The people who knew him and were comfortable with him spoke up; the rest remained silent. He listened—although he often showed annoyance or frustration with their opinions—then made a decision."

It is an all-too-familiar scenario, and one of the major reasons so many people check out mentally during meetings. You will never see it on a great business team because the leader just does not have that kind of gravitas. The nominal leader may continue to run meetings, but he or she does not dominate air time or the decision-making action. Williams says that, when his team reached Stage 4, you would not have been able to easily identify the leader during team meetings. "A strong, effective leader of a high-performing team," notes Williams, "is probably one of the least vocal or energetic people in the room. He or she doesn't hold court, direct the conversation, or make decisions on each agenda item."

On many great teams, there is a different "leader" at each meeting. Some teams rotate the role: If there are eight people, including the leader, on the team, and the team meets once a week, each person will lead a meeting once every eight weeks. Other teams allow the content to determine the leader: Whoever is most—or least—affected by or familiar with the issues to be discussed will lead the discussion. Still others employ the services of an outside facilitator, who "owns" the process of the meeting and keeps the group on track throughout.

How and By Whom Will the Agenda Be Set?

There is an old saying in consulting that he who controls the magic marker controls the meeting. The same can be said about setting the agenda. When Williams' team was in Stage 1, the leader set the agenda for every meeting. When the team got to Stage 4, says Williams, the agenda was "built by the team." That is standard on a great team: Whoever is leading the meeting sets the agenda, with the input of everyone else on the team.

Ken Bloom's experience verifies Williams' team approach to agenda setting. "We were planning a big meeting with all our ocean carriers," Bloom recounts. "When I queried team members about what the objectives of the meeting should be, I got a different answer from each person. Many were unclear about why we were meeting. It wasn't until we all agreed on the objectives that we were able to come up with a tight, meaningful agenda."

A typical agenda for a team's weekly or monthly meetings might include the following:

1. Review of meeting goals.
2. Business update.
3. Progress-check on issues that have been identified in previous meetings; reports of subteams assigned to them; decisions/next steps.
4. Identification of new issues: identify and deploy players who will resolve them; spell out who will be accountable, for what; set timelines.
5. Plan meeting follow up.
6. Agreement on the message(s) the team will convey to the rest of the organization.
7. "How are we doing?" check on protocols.

Note the bias toward action in the agenda. There is no time for the usual FYI round-robin reporting of activities that make typical meetings little more than coma-inducing get-togethers.

Some of the most common complaints about meetings are that they do not get started on time and that the agenda is not circulated in advance. Justified or not, such transgressions are often seen as a sign of disrespect.

As Leigh Ann Errico, a seasoned HR executive with experience at several Fortune 500 global companies, says, "There is never enough time in today's world. The most important rule for meetings is to respect people's time and give them a compelling reason to show up." Regarding time, Errico has seen meeting time cut in half simply by sending out the agenda and relevant attachments several days in advance. This heads-up eliminates the need to spend precious meeting time getting up to speed. As for compelling reasons to show up, Errico stresses the importance of making sure the issues on the agenda are the "big" ones: those that have a real impact on the team's results.

Go Beyond Logistics

The meeting protocols we have just described deal for the most part with logistics: scheduling, room selection and set-up, assignment of responsibilities, and so on. But as Craig Williams points out, "You can be very disciplined and still be dysfunctional. Some Stage 1 and 2 teams have protocols around meeting times, agendas, minutes, etc. But they don't have protocols to address meeting behavior. Protocols are what distinguish a high-performing team."

Here are several behavior-related protocols that great teams insist on:

- The meeting starts on time, with or without you.
- If you can't make a meeting, you send a substitute.
- Cell phones are off; laptops and hand-helds are out.
- There are no digressions from the agenda; if someone raises a new issue, it is "parked" for later discussion.
- There are no side conversations.
- Everyone participates.
- Everyone follows the agreed-upon protocols for conflict resolution.
- All players hold all others—and the leader—accountable for promised deliverables and results.

Remember: Protocols are not eternal laws. They can be revisited, debated, revised, or discarded. Protocols are meant to serve the team, not enslave it.

Issue Management: The High-Performing Way

In our discussion of decision making, we suggested that a newly aligned team invest the time to identify all the decisions that it will need to make before proceeding to make them. The same advice holds for all issues that the team will face: problems it will need to find the cause of, plans it will need to develop and implement, and so on.

At the end of the initial two-day alignment session or shortly thereafter, teams typically develop a comprehensive, specific inventory of all the concerns they will be facing as they work toward their goals. These issues then need to be prioritized so the team can begin working on the most urgent or serious. As the initial set of issues gets resolved, the team adds new ones—the issue-management process is a continuous one.

There are many ways to go about managing key issues. The one outlined here has been adopted by many of the great business teams that we have worked with.

1. *Issue Definition*: In full group, the leader defines and makes visible on an easel the following definition of an *issue*: An *issue* is a threat or opportunity for which some action must be taken by me and/or other members of the team to gain resolution.

2. *Issue Identification*: Team members generate a list of issues confronting the team and/or each of them as a member of the team. The leader captures the discussion and keeps the list visible for the team.

3. *Clarifying Issues*: Team members review the issues to ensure specificity, asking:
   - Is each issue clear and specific?
   - Do issues need to be further divided? (For example, "morale" is too global an issue and might better be divided into subissues, such as: employees in department X are complaining; absenteeism is up; etc.)
   - Is the issue actionable (i.e., is it stated in such a way that an action can be taken)? (For example, "Budget Development" might be more sharply stated as, "We need to improve the annual budget-planning process.")

4. *Priority Setting*: The list of issues is reviewed to identify High, Medium, and Low priorities, by asking:

- What is the *impact* of the issue—on the organization, the team, my department, our competitive position, completion of a mission-critical project, and so on?
- How *urgent* is it?

5. *Action Planning*: The team lays out an action plan for resolution, beginning with the high-priority items. For each issue, the plan includes:

- Selecting a subteam: The smallest number of people required to get closure; it may be just one person.
- Identifying the primary owner of the issue: someone who is process focused, able to depersonalize, has sufficient time, adept at involving others, has access to those required for closure, and so on.
- Determining major steps needed to gain closure.
- Agreeing on key deliverables.
- Establishing timeline/milestones.
- Developing a plan to communicate results to the organization.

One caution about managing issue resolution: Avoid the jump-to-resolution temptation. "List but do not resolve" is a good rule. Dive into resolution only after the action plan has been set. As Helen McCluskey, president of Warnaco Intimate Apparel and Swimwear Group, points out, "The biggest derailer of meetings is that people want to get into the issues immediately. They want to get into the nitty-gritty, the tactical. Whoever is running the meeting needs to prevent that, keep getting the issues down, and park them until the team can go back and decide the best way to tackle each."

Keep It Visible

"Out of sight, out of mind" is a real danger to teams when trying to keep track of issues. Great teams do not allow issues to fall off the radar screen, especially those deemed most serious or urgent. They make sure that, once an issue is identified and an action plan made, it gets resolved, period.

The most efficient way to keep track of issues is to create and maintain an issues log, or list of action items, such as the one that CEO Ken Bloom and his senior management team use at INTTRA. Table 7.1 shows an excerpt from one of that team's recent logs.

O = Original Date
R = Recontracted with SMT Chair

Item	From Mtg	Action Item	Responsibility	Due	Status	Notes
1	11/01/06	Prepare SMT rolling 12-month calendar	TPG	ASAP	Open	
2	11/01/06	Create mechanisms to raise the level of admission for SBOs and increase their level of engagement	TPG/KBB	Ongoing	Open	
3	11/01/06	Document multitier agreements	LBE	O—1/31/07 R—2/28/07	Open	1/30 "Maybe by deadline"
4	01/03/07	Establish policy for forecasting and budgeting software capitalization in 2007; objective is to book on a monthly basis	WJJ	Jan. financials	Closed	
5	01/03/07	Update to Open Requisition Report to include intended recruiting method and related costs	LBE	O—1/31/2007 R—2/13/2007	Open	

Table 7.1 Sample Issues Log

150

INTTRA's log is a very basic one, which is why it works so well. Some organizations go into a great deal more detail, such as a list of people with whom the issue's owner needs to partner or who needs to weigh in. Some include a brief description of the action plan. Others go so far as to identify the people who are likely to get in the way of resolution. Here again, there are no hard-and-fast rules. If it works, then it is right for your team.

Helen McCluskey stresses the importance of updating the log after every meeting and in between meetings if issues are identified outside formal meetings. The updated issues log should be sent out, with the agenda, several days before each meeting so team members can review it, prepare questions, and give some thought to issues that they feel should be added or that need to be addressed.

Another executive we work with makes sure that all the bases are covered when it comes to capturing issues. "In my office," she says, "there is a huge board on which I keep issues visible. There are flip charts. There is always a place to park an issue so it doesn't get lost."

Focus on Accountability

Designating a point person or issue owner for each issue ensures that the job will get done. Each time the issues log is reviewed, there is no hiding out. The point person is fully accountable for reporting on progress—or lack thereof.

Axcan Pharma's CEO, Frank Verwiel, remarks that once he and his team began to follow the issue-resolution model two benefits became immediately apparent: Meetings focused on specific business issues, and at the end of each meeting they decided on next steps, follow-up plans, and so on. Verwiel observes, "People discovered that being held accountable for commitments made during meetings is painful at times, but it adds tremendous value to the process."

Accountability does not mean that you must perform against a commitment *or else*. It can mean coming forward to discuss the need for a midcourse correction, as was the case in an example Verwiel cited: "We were working on a project and in discussions it became clear that the plan that was in place wasn't going to lead to the desired results in the desired time. We decided to go back to the drawing board and redesign the project, adding monthly milestones at which we will check each team member's progress. We are now using these milestones to ensure that we achieve our goals on time. If we hadn't done it, we would have found ourselves in a very difficult situation a year from now."

High-performing teams do not hold people accountable in order to place blame or embarrass people publicly. Accountability is necessary to ensure that results are being achieved. A sensitive leader may choose to first address in private a player's failure to deliver; but if that does not work, or if the failure is commented on in a full meeting, public accountability cannot be avoided. And painful though it may be, addressing the problem publicly is almost always effective.

If the point person fails to step up with full disclosure, then peer-to-peer accountability kicks in. Leigh Ann Errico stresses the importance of addressing the problem head on: "Someone has to say, 'Joe, you owe us the information for the company we are acquiring. We need to know what the costs are going to be. You promised you would have them two days ago. Why haven't we gotten them yet?'"

"You do not really need to point out to people the impact of their failure to deliver; they know what effect it has on results," adds Errico. "But some people need the public reminder of their accountability before they take it seriously."

Accountability is not about blame fixing but about resolving key business issues and achieving results. Without ascending the Accountability Ladder, your team is unlikely to achieve standout performance.

The Promise of High-Performing Meetings

Would any of your colleagues pay to attend a meeting you would be leading? Probably not. Even if you were a high-performing leader, we are not so sure your meetings would command much of an admission price. But should you adopt the concepts proposed in this book, we are certain that your colleagues would show up at your meetings enthusiastically, fully capable, and prepared to contribute. Listen to how some of the executives describe the ways their meetings changed once they began putting these ideas into practice:

- "In Stage 1, no one enjoyed going to meetings; they didn't want to be together. There was tension, you knew there were people not expressing their views and who were playing games about how to position themselves. In Stage 4, it's the reverse. People look forward to meetings. They are comfortable together and trust one another more. Protocols are in place to allow anybody to call anyone else for not putting issues on the table or for creating stories. Issues are not personalized and are rarely unresolved."

  —Craig Williams, Director of Human Resources,
  Johnson & Johnson Vision Care

- "In Stage 4, issues are brought to the table, openly discussed, and everyone has an opportunity to speak. Instead of raising objections after the meeting, people are freer in expressing their views in front of the whole group. Therefore, there is more support for the decisions we have made."

  —Helen McCluskey, President, Warnaco Intimate
  Apparel and Swimwear Group

- "A lot of problems and issues are now solved outside our meetings, by the individuals closest to the action. In our meetings, we spend a lot more time talking about strategic issues and those related to running the business, not putting out fires."

  —Manuel Jessup, Chief HR Officer, Chico's FAS, Inc.

- "Meetings used to be held to inform people, but the real decision making was done outside. Now we have created an environment in which the discussion and decision making goes on in our team meetings. If a person has a contrary point of view, it is voiced in the meeting, not afterwards. If you attended one of our meetings today versus a year ago, you'd see more ideation and optimism, less cynicism, more positive energy around the group."

  —Ray Carson, Jr., Vice President of Global HR,
  Wyeth Consumer Healthcare

- "Perhaps the most dramatic and visible change in the way we work is in our leadership-team meetings. The goal was to become a horizontal team, with each team member equally accountable for the outcome of our decisions. It became very clear that there was no shortage of passion, creativity, and participation, and that my role as leader was becoming much more that of a discussion facilitator than the opinion leader. Besides being more productive now, I think our meetings are actually more fun!"

—*David Greenberg, SVP HR, L'Oréal U.S.A.*

- "At meetings, you would see excellent structure and time management. People would 'begin with the end in mind.' That means you don't go into a meeting just to meet; you go in with a clear goal of what you want to accomplish and by when. These types of meetings have a facilitator—one person who is driving the discussion. Notes are taken and accountabilities acknowledged. People question and challenge one another instead of sitting politely and rolling their eyes. You see laughter and banter, even when the subject matter is challenging and heavy. You see people on opposite sides of an issue walk away together and say, 'We'll work it out.' People are more optimistic because they have some wins under their belt and know that as a team they can deliver. You see people achieving and celebrating success."

—*Leigh Ann Errico, Managing Partner and Executive*
Coach, LA Errico & Partners

Come to think of it, maybe you should begin selling tickets to your next meeting. . . .

Note

1. Lindenberger, Judith. "Make the most of your meetings. . .," *OfficeSolutions,* July 2007.

8 | How Great Teams Communicate

Performance and Language

- mixed messages
- doublespeak
- reports that are high on optimism, low on facts
- excuses
- veiled barbs
- putdowns
- angry outbursts
- ersatz questions (those not intended to elicit information)
- "me first, me only" conversation hogs
- damning with faint praise

Put your ear to the track: How does your team communicate? Do any of the previous items resonate with your team's pattern of communication? Much of what passes as "talk" is really pseudocommunication—it is not intended to authentically present information, a point of view, or even a feeling, but to gain a leg up through ruse, deception, verbal bullying, and finesse. In organizations where the blame game prevails, survival is the first rule of communication. When being questioned or receiving feedback on performance, deny it, make excuses, shift responsibility, pass the buck—in other words, "CYA."

On the other hand, when posing questions or delivering feedback, players on dysfunctional teams favor one of two approaches: either tiptoe around the issue soften the blow, apologize for having to hold the person accountable or, at the other extreme, launch a personal attack, impugn the person's character, or make generalizations based on one incident or shortcoming.

Great teams cannot be bothered with pseudocommunication. They prefer the real thing. When we listen in on the many teams that we have aligned, what strikes us is the consistent pattern of communication that they have in common as they go about meeting business challenges. Here are the 10 common elements that we have found make up the pattern of high-performance communication:

1. *Clarity*. High-performing players demand clarity, not by shouting and screaming "We need greater clarity around here," but by closely questioning one another when an issue is up for discussion or when they have differences of opinion: Can you clarify that? What do you mean by _____? Can you give us an example? What do you see as the consequence? Listening in, you hear these and other clarifying questions—and plenty of them.

2. *Authenticity*. High-performance language sidesteps game playing. You rarely hear team members asking "imposter questions"—those designed to poke holes for the sake of exposing a colleague's Achilles' heel—or making nonrelevant statements just to hear their own voices. High-performance discussion is straight talk. If there is a concern or disagreement, it is put on the table, not hidden under it.

3. *Accuracy*. On a high-performance team, conversation is biased toward facts, data, and observable behavior. You will often hear: "It's my opinion that . . ."—signifying that the speaker wants listeners to

know that he or she is about to enter a no-fact zone—or "On what do you base your judgment?" asking for factual back-up. If a problem is being discussed, the first order of business is to get the facts: What, specifically, is the problem? Where and when is it occurring? Who and how much is involved?

4. *Efficiency.* There is little beating around the bush and verbal foreplay among high performers. Rather than long preambles, you are apt to hear, "John, I have a concern about your behavior, and we need to talk." Excuse-making is a great time waster, which is why the conversation turns away from "It's not my fault" or "If I only had more resources" kind of statements and more toward accepting responsibility and moving on to solutions.

5. *Completeness.* You are unlikely to hear half the story in high-performance environments. What you will likely hear instead is, "Let's discuss the pros and cons of the decision" or "Here are the risks with my proposal, and here's what we stand to gain." The aim is to inform, not to finesse.

6. *Timeliness.* There is a just-in-time feature to high-performing conversations. "Let's put the facts—all of them—on the table, now." One of the favorite questions you'll hear is, "By when?" There is also plenty of "If . . . then" language, often related to the siloless high-performance environment: "*If* Marketing executes its plan by June, *then* Sales will have plenty of time to generate business."

7. *Focus.* On high-performing teams, conversation is typically strictly business, driven by the outcome required in a given situation. If the discussion involves setting priorities for a laundry list of issues, you do not hear anyone jumping into solution mode; if the conversation focuses on *identifying* the root causes of a problem, you are not likely to hear much about taking action to *correct* them. On some teams, there is a good deal of banter and sharp-tongued exchange, but people disagree without being disagreeable. One CEO proudly asserted that on his team, "Insult is the language of affection." But more often it is the source of *affliction*, which is why it is not part of the style of high-performance conversations.

8. *Openness.* High-performance conversations "go there." It is a function of the features common to high-performance teams: no silos but lots of accountability, decision-making protocols, and a focus on results. If a team member—or the leader—is underperforming, or if a function is problematic, colleagues on the team will go there. Dead elephants'

heads—those touchy issues that most teams pretend do not exist—are an endangered species, as was the case when one high-performance team had to make a tough call on a new minority hire—which it did after a frank, fact-based discussion in which no punches were pulled.

9. *Action oriented.* Listen in on a high-performing team at decision time: What are the key objectives? Who are the fewest people who need to be involved? By when should the entire team review the decision? The words connote action. They also typically convey immediacy, as when teams talk about the "24-hour rule." This means getting back to a colleague with a response, if not a conclusion, within one business day.

10. *Depersonalization.* True, high-performing teams "go there," but they do not "go personal." Nor do you hear much defensiveness. Rather, you frequently hear high-performing team members reminding one another in the face of criticism that, "It's a business case." In other words, let us treat the discussion objectively. Another element to depersonalization is that there is little player-to-leader discussion, such as, "Over to you for the decision" or "I'm not sure, what do you think?" And if you watch a team's body language, you don't see more nodding in agreement when the leader speaks than when others voice their opinions.

Like other high-performance behaviors, open communication is an acquired taste and one that works only when you have in place a supportive culture, protocols, and a performance-management system that rewards candor.

The Case for Candor

The philosopher John Stuart Mill wrote compellingly about the importance of dissenting opinions. Dissent helps to sharpen the truth. Mill's insight has not had much impact in many organizations, where boat-rockers are often given the boot. Harvard Business School's *Working Knowledge* points to widespread intolerance of dissenting opinions.[1] Citing examples ranging from the refusal of Detroit's Big Three to take the advice of market researchers to make safer, more-fuel-efficient cars to compete with imports; to NASA engineers who, before the Columbia shuttle disaster, were reluctant to challenge a bureaucracy that ignored safety hazards; to the blind eye that Coca-Cola's decision makers turned when their own managers predicted the failure of "New Coke"—*Working Knowledge* documents the serious consequences of squelching opposing points of view.

HBS Professor Amy Edmondson is of the opinion that the "propensity to maintain silence" is "widespread and problematic in both the public and private sectors."[2] Her belief was reinforced when she and a colleague conducted a survey of over 200 employees, at all levels and in all functions, in a well-known multinational high-tech company:

> We found to a very significant degree that people did not speak up about things they deemed important. Most of those were not "bad news" things; to our surprise we found that people were reluctant to voice what they perceived to be good ideas, unless they were extraordinarily confident they would be well received. And this in a firm that lives and dies by its ideas.[3]

Conflict-averse organizations such as the one Edmondson surveyed can benefit from the example of the legendary Alfred Sloan, according to the *Working Knowledge* article's author:

> At a meeting of one of General Motors' top committees in the 1920s, GM President Alfred P. Sloan, Jr. said, "Gentlemen, I take it we are all in complete agreement on the subject here." Heads nodded around the table. "Then," continued Sloan, "I propose we postpone further discussion of this matter until our next meeting, to give ourselves time to develop disagreement and perhaps gain some understanding of what the decision is all about."[4]

Like GM under Sloan's leadership, the great teams and organizations that we know respect the value of unfettered dialogue. Throughout this book, we cite many examples of team leaders and players who worked hard to overcome their natural inclination to ignore or bury conflict. By acknowledging and dealing with long-avoided dead elephants' heads, these teams entered into a brave new world of honest interaction.

High-performing, horizontal organizations differ from the old hierarchical, command-and-control model in another important way. When it comes to deciding how much information to share, their guiding principle goes beyond the need to *know* to the need to *perform*. Great team leaders realize that the more information their players have, the more effectively they will be able to do their jobs. Ken Murphy— former senior vice president of human resources and administration, Altria Group Inc., and current president of Keltic Ray Creatives, LLC—is one such leader, and he has seen the benefits of sharing information:

> Good leaders treat everyone as though they need to be in the know. They bring the whole team together rather than deal one on one. They encourage the building of the big picture among the whole team, so everyone knows everything. One senior management team I was on spent a whole day, every week, in a room together. There were 10 of us, and we spent the entire day assessing the state of the business, determining strategies for the year, getting updated on one another's work. We framed issues in the form of specific questions. Often those questions began with: How will we … ? We wrestled with tough issues and came up with can-do solutions. We spent a good deal of time together, and the trust that we built up by this intensive cooperation and communication served well when conflict arose.

The Alignment–Clarity Connection

Sometimes the problem is not that conflicts are being suppressed; instead it is that nothing is being discussed. No information is passing between and among the players. Assumptions remain untested; premises go unexamined— it is the ultimate in "don't ask, don't tell" circumspection.

That was the case when Redken's middle managers got together for an alignment. The directors of every department were included. Senior Vice President General Manager Pat Parenty recalls the following conversation:

Sales director to director of marketing: "That printed piece that you send us every month is a bear. We don't know how to use it, nobody looks at it, nobody likes it."

Director of marketing: "What do you mean? We do that because you want it."

Sales director: "We hate it."

Marketing director: "We hate it too, and we spend half a million dollars a year on it."

The two quickly realized that they had not been communicating at all about an expensive tree-waster of a report. They agreed to stop producing it, freeing up a major chunk of the budget for more effective sales and marketing materials. That, says Parenty, was the first of many "wows" that took place during the session.

Alignment provides the structure that facilitates communication in traditionally off-limits areas and enables a team to seek clarity in areas where there has been uncertainty. Confusion about strategy, goals, or responsibilities is a breeding ground for inefficient communication: the need to retreat continually to "Why are we doing this?," and hours spent talking at cross purposes, drawn-out discussions going nowhere. Getting aligned around the five key areas immediately ends the time-wasting and frustration.

In the area of goals, for instance, INTTRA's CEO, Ken Bloom, points out that, "Once you're all in agreement about your purpose, it's easy to articulate what you are seeking. Alignment allows you to dispense with all the pretense and to deliver succinct messages about your expectations and what you want people to do. You have a framework for evaluating one another's goals, priorities, and plans."

Aligning around decision-making protocols also increases effective communication. A few years ago, Wyeth Consumer Healthcare decided to make significant investments in its new-product development group, creating a special "innovation task force" to come up with new ideas and bring as many as possible to market. According to Ray Carson, Jr., vice president of global HR, protocols played an essential role in team communication:

> We started out with ideation teams that brainstormed and came up with about 40 new products, technologies, potential acquisitions that might be commercialized. The innovation team was charged with evaluating the relative viability of each of these. Before we began, we developed a deliberate process through which each idea had to go, and we installed a number of stage gates at which "go–no go" decisions would be made. People knew exactly what to do at each step: who would review the idea at which stage, what kind of information they needed to receive, what would happen if the idea passed, and so on. At each stage gate we evaluate the information we have, make a decision on whether to go ahead, and, if

so, provide some seed funding to gather yet more critical information. It has definitely made us smarter about how we invest money.

Ken Bloom has noticed a hidden benefit from working in a high-performance, aligned environment: increased comfort communicating his ideas. "I have learned how to articulate what I intuit about a business situation," he explains. "I had a hard time learning to articulate that sense, but I can now say what is on my mind more quickly. I realize that being accountable to the company and to my team members requires that I say exactly what I feel and believe, without holding anything back."

Traits of High-Performing Communicators

The act of communication typically involves a message being delivered by one person and received by another. For that communication to be effective, both parties have to be "in sync." The speaker has to be committed to communicating clearly; the listener must make a sincere effort to understand what the speaker wants to convey. Each needs a specific, complementary set of skills, which we explore in depth in Appendix B. Here, we would like to mention just a couple of key traits that characterize high-performing speakers and listeners.

Communication involves implicit and explicit messages. *Explicit* messages are those that hit the auditory hearing apparatus—our ears. *Implicit* messages are the meanings behind the words. These may be conveyed through sound—in the degree of resolve or strength in a statement, for example—but they are also transmitted through body language, posture, eye movements, and so forth. Such messages are not always audible; they are the subtext of communication.

Speakers also find many ways in which to "encode" spoken messages: deliberately remaining ambiguous or using euphemisms and other carefully chosen words. A skilled listener is able to decode the message in spite of these attempts to couch it, and feeds it back to the speaker to ensure that he or she has gotten it right.

High-performing speakers make it easy for listeners; they do not play games or encode their messages. They are careful not to allow *implicit* messages to creep into their communications. They tell it like it is, so the listener does not have to guess at what they mean. Whenever possible, they back up their statements with facts. They refrain from using emotionally charged language. They do not resort to euphemisms or doublespeak.

Penetrating through to the nuance of a message requires an ability to listen with what we referred to in Chapter 4 as the "third ear." Like all good listeners, the coach we described in that example had a keenly developed third ear. This ability, coupled with their acute powers of observation, enables skilled listeners to catch everything: how and where the speaker sits, how he or she dresses, what his or her body language implies. Is the eyebrow arched? Is the speaker turned away or avoiding eye contact? Does he or she seem nervous or reluctant? These are all messages, often as potent as the spoken word.

Chico's Chuck Nesbit saw the need for improved listening when Chico's, which had long been a single-brand company, acquired the White House and Soma brands. The challenge, as Nesbit saw it, was, "As each of the functional specialists became responsible for other brands, they had to get out of the mindset that 'It worked for Chico's, so it will work for White House and Soma.' They had to learn to listen to the people responsible for these businesses."

Replacing the single-brand mentality with an awareness of the different needs of the other brands took time, says Nesbit. It also required skills training to enable people to become better listeners. "The people who failed were those who were not willing to listen and accept that others' ideas had validity. For those who were able to make this leap, the next step was to learn how to have a dialogue and work through the issues together. People who are conflict averse and have built defenses must learn to take them down, remove impediments they have put in the way. They must learn to engage. If they don't have the skills, you have to make sure they get them."

The combination of a speaker who tries in earnest to be as clear and forthright as possible and a listener who possesses the skills needed to pick up any hint of a hidden message is unbeatable. This pairing is why you rarely hear a high-performing team say that, "What we have here is a failure to communicate."

Virtual Communication[5]

The modern business enterprise faces a communication challenge unknown to its predecessors: virtual communication. The faceless, voiceless communication that prevails in the Digital Age is rife with inherent difficulties. Take e-mail as an example.

For those who shy away from confrontation, e-mail provides a perfect out. It lends itself to dealing in data points and deadlines and provides an easy escape for those unwilling to penetrate the emotional subtext of an issue. E-mail also encourages subterfuge. We have seen more than a few executives agonize over an e-mail response, editing and reediting it, secretly circulating the e-mail or intended response to colleagues—often in breach of confidentiality—for feedback, guidance, and perhaps even a little old-fashioned character assassination. E-mail also makes it easy to put forward hidden agendas, such as the need to sing one's own praises or make another person look bad.

E-mail also engenders bravado. The remoteness of the communication process may explain why "scud e-mails," as one executive termed them, are launched with such great frequency.

Face-to-face communication allows the speaker and listener to connect on both the intellectual and physical planes, and it provides the listener with an opportunity to decode and feed back both the content and the emotion of the message. E-mail, on the other hand, makes the utilization of these tools next to impossible. In the black-and-white glare of computer-generated characters, the lyrics may come across loud and clear, but the melody of how the message is spoken and felt is completely lost.

Protocols for the Digital Age

Only the staunchest neo-Luddite would argue that virtual communication is more of a curse than a blessing, but there is no doubt that protocols are essential to harnessing the communication potential of the Internet. In fact, the same rules and protocols that apply to real-life communication need to be incorporated into the team's e-mail etiquette: no subterfuge, no veiled barbs or weasel-wording, no triangulation—a clear and present danger of "blind" copying. In other words, openness, candor, and depersonalization should be exercised during electronic encounters, just as they are in team meetings.

We collected a series of 10 rules of thumb that great teams follow in whole or in part to help them manage virtual communications.

1. *Use the right medium for the message.*

    Because e-mail does not lend itself to situations that require *interactive* communication, many teams have mandated that players use e-mail only for the dissemination of information. It is *unacceptable* to use e-mail to either raise an issue of concern/conflict or to engage in negotiations. For these purposes, the best medium is face-to-face communication; second best is video-conferencing. The telephone is a distant third. Electronic communication? Outlawed!

2. *Substitute* active-reading *for* active-listening *skills.*

    Test your understanding of e-mail messages on two levels, decoding not just the *content* of a message, but also the *emotion* behind it. First, ask, "Is the *content* of this message clear?" Next, step back and take a wide-angle view of the message. Ask, "What are the *underlying feelings* being conveyed or implied? Do I detect frustration, anger, or confusion? If so, are these feelings being directed at me or at my area of responsibility?" Now you are better positioned to respond.

    Feed the messages back to the sender for confirmation. When we read an e-mail message that has been sent to us, we do not have the opportunity to engage in the subtle testing and probing that is possible in real-time discussions. So, before crafting a response, we may need to feed back to the sender both elements of the message—what has been said and what you think was meant—so he or she can confirm that we have gotten it. If the e-mail message you received is really muddled, it might be better not to try to divine the message. Instead, send back an e-mail asking for clarification. Ask questions such as, "What do you mean by _____? Can you be more specific? Can you give me any examples of _____? What else concerns you about _____?"

    Deliver your messages clearly. When you are the sender of an e-mail message, identify the goal of your message. Ask yourself, "What is the purpose of this e-mail? Will it prompt the receiver to think or act differently? Am I communicating to inform or to persuade?" Once you are clear about the goal of your message, you can use the subject line like a banner headline in a newspaper, warming the recipient up with a clear and concise message stating the purpose of your communiqué. But remember: Using an e-mail to express a concern and ask a person to change his or behavior is dicey business. If a face-to-face meeting cannot be arranged, a phone call is preferable to an electronic message.

3. *Practice the Golden Rule.*

Put yourself mentally in front of the computer screen of the recipient. Ask yourself, "How would I react to the message coming across the screen? Would the message be clear? Would I know what action, if any, I was being asked to take? What feeling or emotion would the message be likely to engender in me?" In other words, think before you send.

Part of practicing the Golden Rule is being sensitive to other cultures. When dealing internationally, for example, take care to eliminate Americanisms and colloquialisms from your writing. And if it is afternoon in the country you are writing to, do not start your message with "Good morning."

4. *Respect confidentiality.*

High-performing players *never* pass along a confidential e-mail to anyone not authorized to read it. It is also important to understand that there is no privacy on the Internet: Anything and everything can be discovered with the right tools in the wrong hands. A security breach could result in hackers having access to sensitive materials, and confidential plans can reach the competition through e-mail. *All* sensitive and confidential information should be delivered face to face.

5. *Know when—and when not—to "cc."*

Teams should agree on protocols for keeping others in the "cc" loop. Protocols need to be developed to address the "cc" issue, not only for e-mails sent within the team, but also for messages sent to other managers across functions. When in doubt, reach agreement with those involved before you "cc" and hit "send." Likewise, "cc" people on your e-mail only when it is absolutely necessary for them to be kept informed.

6. *Do not retain a rescuer.*

Just as great teams do not permit face-to-face triangulation or recruitment of supporters, they frown on anyone circulating to a third party an e-mail that he or she has received. They insist that players deal one on one. The one exception: if a player has gotten permission from the e-mail sender to broaden involvement.

7. *Acknowledge the recipient.*

High-performance players look for opportunities to congratulate or thank one another whenever possible, and e-mail can be a very effective medium for delivering positive feedback. One executive we know suggests using e-mail to "bury the hatchet." She has seen situations in which there has been a strained relationship between two people and, when the conflict has eased, one of the parties has sent an e-mail to the other thanking or congratulating the former adversary: "Thanks so much for the work you did on the marketing plan; you and your team were tremendously helpful to us," or "Congratulations! I heard you got the XYZ account." And unlike instances in which people copy others to triangulate or put another person down, in these cases it is totally appropriate to send a copy to other members of the department or unit.

8. *Get to know your e-mail correspondents.*

Electronic communications with team members you have never met in person are often easier when you begin your relationship by sharing a personal detail or two. When you finally do meet, you will have a basis on which to build a good working relationship and, perhaps, a friendship as well.

9. *When in doubt, do not send.*

High-performing teams stress the need for caution when sending e-mail. They recommend that players suspend their responses, especially when they are angry or upset. Waiting 24 hours, then opening and rereading the message can prevent embarrassment and regret.

10. *Pack a parachute.*

Great players are not afraid to bail out of e-mail, especially when they sense the undertow of strong emotion. Before the situation deteriorates—before misunderstandings escalate and harsh messages are exchanged—they suggest getting together by telephone or in person.

Common sense and a few guidelines can help players use digital technology to deliver clear messages, enhance transparency, and keep everyone's eyes focused on customers and competitors, rather than on their computer screens and the next round of "scud e-mails."

End Thought

The great linguist Edward Sapir once pointed to a pattern of *linguistic interinfluencing* that occurs when neighboring people contact one another. They begin to borrow one another's vocabulary and accents. This sharing is a point that applies equally to organizations. To the extent that senior teams talk the talk of high performance and, of course, walk it as well, the rest of the organization is likely to do the same.

Which brings us to our next subject: How to build a great organization made up of great teams on every level.

Notes

1. Emmons, Gary. "Encouraging Dissent in Decision-Making." Harvard Business School's *Working Knowledge for Business Leaders,* October 1, 2007.
2. Ibid.
3. Ibid.
4. Ibid.
5. For a more expansive treatment of the subject of Virtual Communication, see: Guttman, Howard M. *When Goliaths Clash: Managing Executive Conflict to Build a More Dynamic Organization.* AMACOM, 2003, pp. 168–195.

9 | From Great Teams to a Great Organization

Much has been written over the past decade about how to transform an organization through high-voltage and exceedingly complex approaches such as reengineering, renewal, and restructuring—the 3R's of organizational change—not to mention innumerable improvement initiatives ranging from Balanced Scorecarding to Total Quality Management. The approach to organization change taken by high-performing companies is substantially different.

- *First, the vision is a high-performance, horizontal one.* Within teams and then within the organizational context in which they operate, the thrust is to break down hierarchies, eliminate silos, distribute decision making, and create a sense of "we accountability" throughout the organization. And the requirement is for leaders to go horizontal for real, beginning with their team and their ability to transform it into a mini board of like-minded, high-performing leader-players. Perhaps the best description of a high-performance, horizontal organization comes from Robert Gordon, CEO and managing director, Dairy Farmers of Australia. This definition was quoted previously but is worth repeating:

A horizontal organization . . . [is one] in which everyone operates according to a clearly defined set of decision-making protocols, where people understand what they are accountable for and then own the results. It means moving to an action- and results-driven workforce at every level—not one that waits around for instructions or trips over functional boundaries. It means giving employees the opportunity and skills to decide who needs to be involved in solving problems and making decisions, dividing responsibilities, then stepping aside to allow people to implement.

- *Second, the goal is squarely on business results.* Change per se is not a key objective of the high-performing approach. Instead, the fuel for the effort is a significant business challenge that must be met. What matters is accelerating performance to achieve a high measure of results. There is no gap between the change effort itself and the business results it seeks to produce.
- *Third, the focus is on tight targeting.* High-performing leaders shy away from large-scale interventions aimed at transforming entire organizations in relatively short order. They set their sights on the molecular level of organizational life—the performance and interaction of teams and their members. Their rationale is simple: Since teams are the basic work unit of the modern enterprise, the transformation process must start with them. Transform teams, ideally beginning with the senior management team, and business results will follow.
- *Fourth, the emphasis is on building organizational momentum.* The high-performing approach to change begins with the senior team—whether at corporate, divisional, business unit, or even departmental level. Once the alignment process takes hold on a team, the transformation is immediate and highly visible. It becomes readily apparent in the behavior of team members: in how they view themselves and

engage players on the team, their direct reports, and their colleagues. The change shows up in everything from their riveting focus on achieving results to the way they go about building business relationships based on authenticity and honest confrontation. As you align teams throughout the organization—tier to tier and team to team—you create a "how do we get into the club" kind of momentum. As the process unfolds in a carefully structured and sequenced approach, the organization becomes a high-performing, horizontal entity.

The Five Musts for Building Great Organizations

An $8 billion European consumer products company, a division of a global leader in the industry, faced an uncertain future. Growing competition, shorter product life cycles, mounting costs and shrinking profits, finicky customers, and new European-wide government regulations all posed major threats. The senior team realized that the old way of operating, in which each successive tier in the organization managed the tier below, led to a downward focus throughout the organization. Executives were absorbed in fire-fighting and the details of execution rather than spending time on crucial strategic issues.

The top team moved to put in place worldwide, high-performance business teams, each responsible for setting strategy and resolving key operational issues. The team approach was eventually cascaded down throughout the organization. In the new situation, the senior team operated like a board of directors, focusing on company-wide strategic issues, capital markets, and longer-term business growth and return. As a result, the performance of those at succeeding levels rose to a much greater level of impact, as teams and units everywhere stepped up to greater levels of responsibility and authority. Cycle time was reduced; innovation at all levels improved measurably; turnover declined; people felt a greater level of commitment; and the growth trajectory continued.

Among other things, the new approach trigged an unexpected change in career planning. Employees' thinking gradually shifted from the traditional technical-versus-managerial vertical tracks to a more horizontal consideration of participation on business teams. The high-performance team had become a powerful force for wider cultural and organizational change.

A top-to-bottom high-performing organization is an ambitious goal, but one well within the reach of every leadership team committed to the change. As you think about moving to a new leadership and operating model for your organization, consider the following five requirements for success.

1. Keep It Simple, Stupid!

K.I.S.S.—an acronym to the wise, as anyone in the field of organization development will tell you. But simplicity is a virtue that is more often preached than practiced. The problem is that organizations today do not have the luxury of undertaking one of those late 20th-century transformation initiatives that cost time, money, and resources with little or no return on investment. One reason that the high-performing, horizontal team model is so effective is its innate simplicity.

Prior to its reorganization into global category teams, Novartis OTC had been structured along geographical lines, with brand teams in each region. There was a global marketing group, a global R&D function, and individual global brands; but each region was basically a stand-alone entity, given to the insular silo thinking typical of geographically segmented environments.

CEO Larry Allgaier led Novartis OTC's change to a high-performing organization. In our initial meeting, he listened skeptically as I described what the undertaking would entail, beginning with his senior team and then cascading the model down to the category teams and other critical functional and cross-functional teams within his organization. "Where's the magic in this?" he asked me. "It's so simple, how can it work?"

Two meetings later Allgaier saw the light. A good deal of the magic lies in the simplicity of the approach. "I began to understand the power," Allgaier says, "that comes from changing how you interface with one another. These are all things you know you *should* do, but don't. When you finally begin to work in an atmosphere of high respect, high accountability, and protocols, you can put tough issues on the table and work through them transparently. That makes all the difference."

In our experience, organizations that have succeeded in going horizontal take a direct, straightforward path. Their leaders ask: What do we have to do to prepare us to meet a current business challenge and those that lie ahead? Are the leadership teams—and other teams whose involvement is required—up to the challenge? If not, what must be done to raise the level of performance?

The alignment process recognizes the importance of compatible structures, systems, and processes. Barriers in these areas must be identified and eliminated; doing so is part of the alignment process. But at the outset of the change process these are not the most difficult barriers to overcome. The showstoppers relate to human interaction: how leaders and team members view themselves, individually and as a team; how they perform; and how they engage those around them in making decisions and resolving issues.

In working through the changes, the focus remains squarely on business issues. The approach is simple and direct, and it connects, in real time, change, learning, and issue resolution. It is learning—and transforming—by doing.

2. Leaders Must Lead

The initial impetus for change at Novartis OTC came from the chief marketing officer, Philippe Zell. He presented a persuasive case for changing the way category teams worked and interacted with one another. But how could these teams be expected to become aligned and interdependent if the division's Global Leadership Team was not?

Realizing that top management's support was crucial, Zell reached out to CEO Larry Allgaier who, along with his Global Leadership Team, became the force for broader organizational change. Just over a year into the change, the top team's leadership has proven decisive to the early success achieved by Novartis OTC.

Readers of the previous chapters know that operating horizontally represents a radical departure from the hierarchical comfort zone. It requires making private, internal changes—not just organizational ones. Rob Gordon is a man passionately committed to the kind of change we are discussing. But he also knows that change begins with him. I remember how in the early stages of the alignment process he encouraged his team to take greater risks, become more transparent, work more interdependently, and hold one another accountable. He solicited input from his team regarding how he could become a more effective force for change both *within* the team and *for* the organization. He listened carefully to suggestions and accepted feedback in a depersonalized way. One hundred years after Dairy Farmers' inception—and under Gordon's leadership—the company is poised to become a high-performance, horizontal organization driven to achieve significantly higher levels of performance.

Along with a determined, committed leader, the top management team must also live the *eight attributes* of every stage 4 high-performance team:

1. clear team goals
2. right players in place
3. clear roles/responsibilities
4. commitment to winning for the business over self-interest
5. agreed-upon protocols for decision making and conflict resolution
6. sense of ownership/accountability for business results
7. comfort dealing with conflict
8. periodic self-assessment

If the change to a high-performance, horizontal organization does not begin with the top leader and his or her leadership team, there is no point in continuing the process. Greatness is just not in the cards.

3. Talk It Up—and Down—and Every Which Way

The alignment process begins with an overview session in which the leader presents the business case for change, much in the manner of what we saw John Doumani do in Chapter 4. It is Step One in the process by which the leader enrolls his or her team, allays fears, and begins the momentum.

If there is skepticism and anxiety among senior team members, expect these to increase exponentially at succeeding levels. As the high-performance, horizontal vision is carried to an ever-widening circle of teams, there is a need to foster understanding, lessen fear, and create energy.

There is no one right way to do this. The high-performing process varies situationally. For example, in some organizations the alignment overview session includes not just the leader and the top team, but also that team's direct reports—"Tiers 1 and 2," respectively, in the parlance of many organizations. During the session, the members of Tier 2 learn what Tier 1 will be experiencing and why; what the impact will be on Tier 2 players; and what to expect when their turn comes. However it is done, the effect of an alignment overview session is immediate and profound. Any team within arm's length of a newly aligned team must be brought into the circle.

At INTTRA, CEO Ken Bloom deliberately rolled the process down to the level below his senior management team in a quick, bold stroke that did not even allow his direct reports to fully absorb the high-performing concepts. His rationale: Squeezed by both downward and upward pressures, the senior team's performance would not have anywhere to go but up.

Smaller companies or business units sometimes elect to include in the alignment overview session all employees—or at least all those who serve/are likely to serve on any team in the organization. This inclusion demystifies the process from the outset, is likely to dispel rumors about the proposed changes, and gives everyone an opportunity to raise questions.

There are many opportunities to communicate as the initiative unfolds. One of these chances comes at the end of each alignment session, when the newly aligned team thinks through what it wants to communicate about the session to its direct reports and any other colleagues. For example, at Novartis OTC, one category team went through the initial alignment session and concluded that its message to the next tier should be as follows.

- The purpose of our alignment was to set expectations and clarify roles/goals of team members in the cold-cough-respiratory category.
- Key outcomes of our alignment were:
  - the drafting of this year's Objectives/Goals, Strategies, and Measures for the category
  - a deeper understanding of the roles and responsibilities of the team members
  - the identification of questions and issues that need to be answered/resolved
  - the creation of protocols for decision making, conflict resolution, and so on.
- What is in it for you?
  - more focus and direction
  - transparency and clarity on how this team will operate
  - everyone working at higher efficiency
  - an opportunity to unleash your energy

The Novartis OTC category team wisely included a "what's in it for you" set of messages. Unless you can tie change to self-interest, communication remains just talk, without much impact.

4. Do What Works

After the top team—Tier 1—is aligned, there are a number of ways to introduce the high-performance model to the rest of the organization. The organization's needs should dictate the sequence in which high-performing teams are replicated.

One approach is a "multi-tier" alignment. This is very carefully done— and only after Tier 1 has been aligned, gained skills, and been reassessed to ensure that it is tracking as a Stage 3 or 4 team. At this point, Tier 1 is aligned with its direct reports in Tier 2. Typically, Tier 2 is then given time to get up to speed and is then aligned with Tier 3. The process then continues to cascade through the organization.

For a variety of reasons, some organizations opt to move from the alignment of Tier 1 to functional alignments. This was the case in Liz Claiborne's Special Markets Business. As Lisa Piovano Machacek—vice president of human resources for Liz Claiborne, Inc.—explains, "This was an interim step taken by senior managers who were not quite ready to move directly to a new, cross-functional brand-team structure. While planning the changeover, putting each of the functions through an alignment paved the way for the move to the horizontal structure and prepared people for their new roles and responsibilities."

Mark Stevenson, executive vice president of Applied Biosystems (AB), recalls Cathy Burzik's efforts to create a great organization when she became president of AB. She began by aligning her senior team. We have previously discussed that team's success in breaking down silos, learning to operate like a mini board of directors, and pushing decision making down to subteams in order to increase the speed and quality of decisions. Burzik then tried to follow the multi-tier model to cascade high-performance teams down through AB. But she soon encountered problems. As Stevenson remembers, "Initially, we tried to involve all the senior team's direct reports—about 150 in all. But the group was just too large, and there weren't enough common problems for them to work on together." Stevenson points to two other approaches that were more successful. Within each function, high-performing teams were created; high-performing individuals were also pulled in to make up cross-functional teams charged with working on a number of high-priority business issues. Comments Stevenson, "You need to have real issues to deal with in order to go through an alignment. Especially when it comes to conflict resolution, you can't do it unless there are real relationship issues on the table."

Burzik agrees with Stevenson's assessment. When we spoke to her, shortly after she had moved into the top spot at Kinetic Concepts Inc. (KCI), she told us that she had no intention of trying to conduct multi-tier alignments, one after another, at KCI. "I plan to start by aligning the top team, of course, but then I am going to identify key teams below the top team that will be critical to the future success of the company," says Burzik. For example, Burzik quickly realized that KCI needed to establish a global team—consisting of senior, high-producing marketing and R&D leaders—to own the brand for its flagship advanced woundcare product, Vacuum Assisted Closure, or V.A.C.®, therapy. She will give them a mission and then get them aligned. Outside V.A.C. therapy, Burzik had already created a team with strategic focus and another with operational focus, both of which were also aligned around a common mission. She envisions at KCI about 5 teams, of 10 individuals each, that will work on critical issues. These 50 people will be aligned with the top team. "Once this is done," explains Burzik, "there will be consistent, high-performance behaviors across all the teams."

When it comes to creating great teams throughout KCI, Burzik, like all great leaders, does not claim to have all the answers. "The rest of the organization is definitely not going to 'languish.' Over time, we will work proactively to identify the right way to transmit the high-performing message to them."

5. Create a High-Performing Culture

Take Stock of Your Values   *Culture*, anthropologists tell us, is the pattern of norms, values, and beliefs held by societies and groups within them. Some of these norms, values, and beliefs are *explicit*—set forth in corporate manifestos or mission and value statements. Others are *implicit*—not formally espoused, but nonetheless influencing how day-to-day business is conducted.

Whether implicit or explicit, culture can either promote or retard the march toward high performance. Johnson & Johnson's "Credo" is a classic example of a set of explicitly stated beliefs that have driven a company to excel. Published by company founder Robert Wood Johnson in 1943, this one-page document, which states the company's commitment to putting customers first and stockholders last, has guided J&J through good times and bad. Remember the TYLENOL® crises of 1982 and 1986, when the product was adulterated with cyanide, resulting in a number of deaths? Company managers and employees made countless decisions that were inspired by the philosophy embodied in the "Credo," resulting in the preservation of the company's reputation and the rebounding of its TYLENOL® business.[1]

Yet there are implicit norms within J&J that have the potential to inhibit high performance. As one executive pointed out to us, there is an informal tradition of "niceness" among J&J employees—avoiding confrontation and minimizing criticism. No one can argue against niceness but, when it devolves into lack of transparency or an unwillingness to make the tough calls, then virtue becomes a performance vice.

One way to speed up the move to the high-performance model is to focus on the explicit and implicit cultural drivers of performance that are embedded in the organization.

Begin by asking: How can we reinforce existing positive cultural values, such as a focus on results; a horizontal orientation; the willingness to be held accountable, to confront, and to be transparent; and other attributes of high-performance teams and players? Next, ask: What implicitly held values need to be brought to the surface, examined, and, if need be, modified or put aside? Some common inhibitors include niceness that gets in the way of candor; the tendency to overanalyze; a focus on consensus decision making; risk aversion; and the like.

Build on the positive and eliminate the negative aspects of your existing culture in order to create a robust culture of high performance throughout your organization.

Be a Role Model   Great leaders determined to create great organizations know that they must serve as poster-executives for the change. As Ken Bloom explains, "If I don't start meetings on time, the people who report to me won't; if I can't articulate our commercial goal, they won't be able to; if I brook variation in our financial strategy, there will be variation in the implementation of that strategy." Bloom is so aware of his responsibility in this area that he had INTTRA's offices remodeled, and every wall is now made of glass. "I know everyone is always looking at my behavior. The glass walls are a constant visual reminder that I should only be spending my time on critical issues; they have made me constantly vigilant about what is on my desk and what I am doing at the moment."

Bloom has learned that, if he really walks the talk, then rule by CEO whim is not an option. Having committed publicly to a certain strategy, he cannot walk into Marketing and say, "Let's start an alliance program." Strategic inconsistency is not a mark of high-performing leaders. Does he mind the constraint? "When we began this initiative, we were processing 18,500 containers a week," he answers. "I was concerned that we didn't have the management discipline to be able to process 36,000 a week. We are now doing over 200,000 a week. Our growth is continuing; our retention rate is 98 percent. Ask me again if I mind."

Continue to Communicate   The need to communicate about the high-performance effort never ends; in fact, it grows as more teams are aligned and begin using the ideas. Bloom's senior team spends the last few minutes of its monthly meeting crafting the message it wants to send to the rest of the organization, including a list of the decisions it has made and the rationale for them. Scott Edmonds' Tier 1 team at Chico's meets once a week, and a member of Tier 2 is always present to take notes that he or she then transmits to the rest of that tier. And after each reassessment that these teams go through, they report to the next tier on their progress.

Marc Robinson, who was president of Pfizer Consumer Healthcare and, after its purchase by Johnson & Johnson, is now company group chairman, says that each time the division's quarterly results were released to the public he chaired an all-colleague meeting. He reported on their annual-goals progress, emphasizing the importance of everyone in the company continuing to follow the principles of high performance, as individuals and team members. "We probably overcommunicated," reflects Robinson, "but I believe that is generally the best way of operating."

Did it pay off? "Just look [at] the results we got. Growth was strong; new product success and the percent of revenue from new products were at an all-time high; our scores on annual innovation surveys were very robust," answers Robinson.

Do not forget new hires. They need to be acculturated. Why not begin at the beginning, with the initial interview? For example, during the interview process for new executive hires, Scott Edmonds personally talks to candidates about their values and those of Chico's, and what to expect in a high-performance, horizontal organization. Under the direction of Chief HR Officer Manuel Jessup, an integration process has been put in place, including an off-site meeting at which all those who have been hired in the previous six months are integrated into the horizontal initiative.

Celebrate—and Reward—Success   Any performance-management system worth its salt has carefully thought-out rewards and recognition built into it. Providing positive consequences for high-performance behavior is key to keeping it alive.

Scott Edmonds publicly recognizes people who are authentic champions of high-performance principles. Quarterly, he assembles 1,000 employees outside Chico's Florida headquarters and briefs them on progress. He shares examples of when and where individual employees exhibited high-performance behavior. He calls each of them up on the stage with him and talks about how their actions have demonstrated that they understand and practice high-performing principles. Small accomplishments—whether refusing to participate in triangulation, observing the 24-hour rule of "resolve it or drop it," or holding one's team leader accountable—are celebrated alongside big successes.

Recognition is a great motivator, but rewards are a sure-fire way to ensure that desired behavior continues. At INTTRA, between 40 and 60% of employees' performance ratings are based on their team behaviors: Are they candid; do they avoid nonassertive or aggressive behavior; do they honor commitments, accept responsibility, and deliver and receive feedback in the right spirit? Percentages vary from one organization to the other, but results are the same: pay for high performance keeps performance high.

Make It Visible   Numerous studies have been done on the effectiveness of subliminal messages. Even when we are not conscious of receiving messages, cues around us are delivering them. Placing reminders throughout the workplace is another way of ensuring that the high-performance principles continue to be reinforced.

Organizations can do this in a number of ways. Many keep lists of agreed-upon protocols posted in meeting rooms. At the entrance to Scott Edmonds' office, there is a big sign that says, "I Practice HPTs

(High-Performance Teams)." Inspired by Edmonds, some Chico's employees have taken to wearing HPT bracelets. And Chico's, Mars Inc., INTTRA, and several other companies have produced and circulated pamphlets that summarize the principles of high-performance and stress the commitment to them.

Building a Great Organization the Redken Way

When L'Oréal bought Redken USA in 1993, the brand had slipped from number one in hair-color sales to number three or four. L'Oréal brought in a new management team made up of a senior vice president and a number of vice presidents. Aimed at reviving Redken's fortunes, the raft of initiatives they came up with—from advertising strategies to communication vehicles to new product development—went nowhere. What defeated the team, perhaps more than anything else, was the conflict among its members. As Pat Parenty, Redken's current SVP and general manager, points out, "You can't get the work done if you are dealing with infighting all the time."

Four years later, despite the flurry of effort, not much had changed in terms of Redken's overall market position and bottom line. In 1997, Redken's top team had had enough. It decided to make a radical shift to the high-performance, horizontal model.

Immediately after the initial alignment session, things changed. Some players on the senior team were replaced. The VP of sales departed and Parenty took his place. As roles and responsibilities were clarified, it became obvious that much of the decision-making power resided with the SVP. The issue was quickly addressed. Candid feedback to the SVP, once frowned upon, now flowed. When the SVP retired, Parenty took over the reins.

A great senior team does not make a great organization, which is why Parenty and his team decided to cascade the high-performance model down to the second tier: the company's 25 directors. The senior team carefully laid the groundwork. After their alignment, the members of the senior team briefed the directors ("We didn't provide the gory details," explains Parenty, "just the bottom line"), attended director's meetings, and kept ongoing discussion focused on the transformation. By the time the Tier 2 alignment session was held, the director-level executives were ready, willing, and able.

Well, not quite *able*. As typically occurs, a gap analysis conducted at the conclusion of the Tier 2 alignment revealed that the directors needed a skills upgrade. Over the next several months, they participated in a care-fully constructed training regime aimed at providing them with the critical leadership, conflict-management, and influencing skills required for them to play at new, high-performing levels.

As a result, the senior team and the directors began to work together more seamlessly. Collaboration improved. Respective roles and responsi-bilities were clarified, which led to rooting out overlaps and redundancies. Underground behavior became a thing of the past. Decisions between the two tiers were made faster and more effectively.

Next up were the 100 or so managers who reported to the directors, and once they were aligned the process was repeated until all managers and field personnel were aligned in what Parenty describes as "an organiza-tion-wide evolution toward the practice of high-performing teams." The effort was completed three years ago, and as new employees come aboard there is a structured process designed to increase the likelihood that they will be enthusiastic adopters from day one.

Did the trek from great senior team to great organization pay off? You be the judge:

Bottom Line

By 2007, Redken had achieved 10 years of double-digit sales and profit growth—a record no other hair care company has matched in the last decade.

Organization

Roles and responsibilities have become clearly delineated, eliminating interdepartmental tugs of war. For example, Education and Sales once worked at cross-purposes: There was no clear agreement about who did what to one another—or to the customer. Important issues were left unattended. Today, the confusion is gone; both functions work hand in glove, presenting customers with a powerful and integrated sales-education approach.

Decision delay has been replaced by a clear decision-making pro-cess. In the old days, there was a good deal of back-and-forth jostling at the outset of decisions. Whose call was it? Who should be involved? How many approvals were needed? Now, everyone knows which major decisions will be made at each level and who will make them. When there is a stalemate, the decision is elevated to the next level. If disagreement persists, the decision lands on Parenty's desk. "That rarely happens," he comments, "because someone, somewhere has been empowered to decide; everyone knows who it is; that person takes responsibility and makes the decision."

People

There is no hiding out. People no longer hesitate to admit a mistake. You fess up and move on. "In this model," says Parenty, "you depersonalize; you don't attach the issue to a person." Mistakes are no longer career-enders, unless of course you are a serial offender. "Because there are no repercussions, it makes it easier for the issue to be resolved," Parenty concludes.

Teams

Teams throughout the organization attack the priorities—those that come from the business strategy. If the marketing team is considering launching a program to find new users, the opening question is: Is that within our business strategy? If "yes," the team moves quickly to the next level of discussion: What is our current method? How would this new method compare—and can we win competitively? What are the measurables? Who is driving the decision? If the program gets the go-ahead, the team proceeds just as quickly to determine who is responsible for each area and how much responsibility the full team, a subteam, and/or individuals will have for resolution. Cycle time from idea to implementation has been cut dramatically.

Customers

Communication to customers has become more focused and on point. Ask Redken customers about a new offer—a new hair care product, for example—from the company and you will be amazed at how well-informed they are. Salon owners know whom the program is targeted to, why Redken believes it will work, what all the components are, what they need to do to execute it, what Redken's support will be, what their role will be, what the costs will be, and so on. They understand the logic behind what is being done. "You wouldn't get that same clarity from another company," says Parenty proudly.

Redken field professionals are viewed by customers not as product pushers, but as strategic thinkers and partners. Comments Parenty, "We show up as long-term strategic thinkers and planners. We don't show up on Friday and ask them to do something on Monday. We go in, we say, 'Part of our year-long business plan for you is to help you achieve this goal, and here is how we would like to work together to get there. It requires training, here's what we'll provide. It requires promotion, here's our plan, etc.'"

Customers know exactly whom they are supposed to work with on each element of the plan. They know where to go to get answers clearly and quickly. They view Redken as an organization that knows what it is doing. "A frequent comment from our customers," says Parenty, "is 'You guys are all on the same page.'"

End Thought

At the end of the day, companies stand or fall on what happens at the moment of customer interface: the five feet of space between them and their customers, voice-to-voice telephone conversations, or, increasingly, the click of a computer. The high-performance model not only redefines how an organization is led and run, but how it behaves in the marketplace as well. Great organizations build great customer relationships.

While the high-performance, horizontal approach is complexity averse, it is not a cakewalk. There are obstacles and challenges along the way, which is the theme of our concluding chapter.

Note

1. http://www.jnj.com/our_company/our_credo_history/index.htm; jsessionid=0GAP0O0XUQXH4CQPCCFWU2YKB2IIWTT1

10

Great Leaders and Teams: Challenges, Responses, and Remaining Issues

Little in life is as easy as it seems—or reads—especially in books on management. Our aim in this chapter is to briefly identify a number of the key challenges that we have seen high-performing players and teams face, share some of the insights we and they have gleaned in grappling with these challenges, and point to gaps and unanswered questions that require further thought and action.

Challenge: Overcoming Resistance to Change

In *War and Peace,* Leo Tolstoy raises the question: What would prompt a young man to put life and limb on the line by following a leader into war? The question remains as relevant today as it was back in Tolstoy's day. It is one of those fundamental questions that cut to the essence of human behavior: What prompts people to do what they do? Why do they behave in a certain way? What causes them to overcome fear and inertia to follow some new, untraveled path?

We do not pretend to have the answers to these deep and complex questions, even if we relate them to the narrower slice of organizational life. We surely do not have scientifically valid answers as to how organizations can change the behaviors of those who show up each day in varying states of readiness, willingness, and ability to shift paradigms and routines.

What we can offer are practical tips—a kind of results verification—that come from great leaders who have successfully overcome resistance to change to take their teams to a very different place.

Be Reassuring

Fear is a basic human emotion. It is difficult for people to embrace your vision of some new tomorrow, no matter how brightly you paint it, when they remain frozen in fear. Safety first! is a powerful imperative—all the more so in the wake of the never-ending layoffs, cutbacks, and outsourcing of the last decade. Not surprisingly, change, with all the uncertainty attached to it in leaner times, breeds fear.

Managing the fear of change is a top priority for high-performing leaders, who know that "greatness" requires making deep organizational and personal change. This is where Grant Reid—global president of Mars Drinks, whom we followed in Chapter 2—proved to be such an effective leader. When Reid was faced with the challenge of turning around sales at Mars's Snack unit, the first thing he did was head directly to associates—especially those whose leader had been replaced by Reid—to reassure them.

Reid set up one-on-one meetings with his VPs and their direct reports to explain his vision for the future and ask for their help in achieving it. He encouraged them to express their feelings about the changes by asking questions such as: How are you feeling? What are you thinking about your future here? What are your major concerns?

Listening to the answers, Reid realized that people wanted reassurance that their futures were secure. It is one reason why he carefully explained what was going to change and what their roles would be going forward. He let people know the end game; let them know they would have a hand in bringing it about; and tested for commitment. He also assured his newly acquired staff that he was not going to give preferential treatment to those who reported to him in the past. By explaining to his associates just what was going to change and how it was going to affect them personally, Reid was able to allay their fears and gain their commitment.

Dealing with the psychological subtext of change is a necessary condition for overcoming resistance to change, but managing the organizational context is also important. Are all the elements of the performance-management system—everything from goal clarity to feedback to skills to rewards—all working together to encourage people to move in the new direction?

Bottom-line lesson for leaders: Keep in mind that change does not just happen—it happens *to people*.

Pace Change

Assume that your people can only deal with one significant change at a time. Change is a fact of life. "You can't step into the same river twice," said Heraclitus in 500 BCE. And he had not even heard of Future Shock, "versioning" product strategies, and Moore's Law! Do not expect *hurrahs* when you announce the move to the new high-performance, horizontal model.

One way to keep Future Shock from undermining your efforts to "go horizontal" is to make sure that people have sufficient time to understand and absorb the change—and plenty of opportunity to ask questions. The ability to deal with change varies from one person to the next. As Axcan Pharma's CEO, Frank Verwiel, reminds us, "It's a challenge to strike the right balance between getting people to change enough to make a difference and not making so many changes that they become paralyzed."

There is no formula for finding that balance. High-performing leaders know how to carefully weigh the business case for the change and its urgency with how far the organization must travel to get there. They also know how to convey to everyone that moving horizontally is the "real deal," rather than just another ersatz, this-too-shall-pass initiative.

Tie in Self-Interest

Change to some extent involves balancing consequences. People are more apt to change when there are incentives to do so—and disincentives for clinging to old habits. What will the high-performing model mean in terms of how players in an organization earn their livings and live their professional lives? What is the cash value to them? What are the rewards in terms of their careers, their ability to operate freely, to tap their creative energy, and to express themselves freely without all the task interference of a siloed, hierarchical environment?

Brian Camastral, regional president of Latin America for Mars, Inc., is a superb consequence thinker—a skill that he uses adeptly in managing high-performance change. Imagine, he challenged his change-shy team members, if we could create a situation in which each of the decentralized geographical units could work together as an area-wide team, continue to operate independently, and yet improve individual unit results.

Camastral got his team's attention. He then made the business case for aligning each unit's strategy with Mars' global strategy. Camastral took his top team through an alignment session, which barreled home the point that with each unit working off the same strategic plan, parts would be more interchangeable, allowing for cross-border mutual assistance. Executives on his team realized that they would remain accountable and be rewarded for their unit's results, not the region's—but their unit's results would improve, given a freer flow of talent. "The attitude began to shift," says Camastral, "until everyone wanted to be on the winning team, and they were all determined to make it work, individually and collectively."

We have talked throughout this book about the need to leverage off a "burning platform"—a compelling business issue—as a springboard for change. How about the need for a burning *personal* platform? Remember Paul Parker, vice president of HR for Colgate-Palmolive's (CP's) Africa-Middle East Division, and his South African team of "mavericks?" The team enjoyed the rough-and-tumble of the local marketplace. The only problem: The region wanted to play a more robust corporate role and become a global supplier for CP, which it could not do if it remained at its current level.

Enter the company need/individual self-interest nexus. When it was pointed out to the South Africans that the behaviors they could get away with in that particular marketplace did not play well on the global level, the players began to realize they were never going to be viewed by corporate as a source of talent for the global organization. For the first time they asked themselves, "How do we accelerate our careers within CP?" The answer: "By demonstrating high-performance behaviors." Which they began to do.

Then there is that not-so-subtle, but highly effective, stand-by carrot: Pay for team performance. Many companies now reward both results *and how they are achieved*. In one company we know, a full 40% of compensation depends on "soft" behaviors: authenticity, following protocols, depersonalizing, holding others accountable, being receptive to feedback. And rewarding these behaviors really helps people take that leap of faith onto a new path.

Challenge: When the Team Gets a New Leader

Lifetime employment with one company? Do not count it, especially if you are the CEO. Annual turnover of CEOs around the globe increased by 59% between 1995 and 2006. In 2006, global CEO turnover averaged 14.3%, and the average tenure of a CEO was only 7.8 years.[1] How do organizations remain great in the face of this challenge?

The departure of a CEO or any C-suite player is usually an unsettling event for a company. But great leaders are just as adept at *leaving* teams as they are at *leading* them. Cathy Burzik's departure from Applied Biosystems is a good example. Several months after Burzik left AB, we asked Mike Schneider, then-president of the company's Global Services Division, what impact her departure had. His answer? "Much less than you'd expect when a typical CEO departs."

If we had asked Schneider the same question the day he learned that Burzik was leaving, he would have given a very different response. "I was driving to the airport when I received a call from a coworker in England informing me that Cathy had resigned," recounts Schneider. "Life as I knew it at AB had come to an abrupt end. I thought the stock market was going to kill us, and the positive momentum we were enjoying was also coming to an end. The leadership team arranged a conference call early that same day, and everyone was trying to figure out what we needed to do to recover, how to keep this positive momentum going. But within a week we all came to the realization that it was all of us working as a cross-functional team that had created the upside we were enjoying, and we knew we had the ability to continue down that path."

When we asked Burzik what she had done to prepare her team for her departure, it became apparent that this "nonevent" actually took some significant orchestration on her part. "I thought hard about what I could do to accelerate them, to make them stand strong and on their own," she explains. "I purposely extricated myself more and more from day-to-day business operations. I was still very involved in leading the strategic team, but we had created horizontal teams throughout the company. They were running the business, and my team was running them. I knew that once I left, the members of my team would be interacting with the Board of Directors more, so I began coaching them, saying things like, 'Think about how you would present this recommendation to the board.' I also tried to give them increased visibility at board level instead of my always being the one to interact with the board."

Mark Stevenson, president of AB's Molecular Cell Biology Division, sums it up quite well. "Ultimately," he says, "Cathy prepared us by having transformed us into a high-performing team."

The impact of a great leader cannot be exaggerated, even though the high-performing model does away with leader dependency. Burzik's departure was not disruptive because, when she turned around to leave her organization, what she left behind was a team of leaders willing and able to step up to a higher level of responsibility.

Challenge: When the Leader Gets a New Team

It is one thing for a high-performing CEO to pack his or her bags and head for a new corner office. Typically, that CEO has plenty of room to bring the revolution to the new organization. But what about great vice presidents, managing directors, department heads, and other team leaders who join a new organization intending to ratchet up performance the same way they did in their previous position? Returning to a hierarchical environment is not an easy task. How does such a leader create a pocket of high-performance within an organization that does not "get it?"

In observing high-performing individuals attacking new roles, our caution is: Do not try to conquer the world; start in your immediate area. This is how Leigh Ann Errico, former pharmaceutical HR executive, sees it. "If it is within your control, just do it. You can't say, 'This is a hierarchical company, so my area will be that way, too.' Make it happen and worry about the rest of it later. We have to change what we can, get our own house in order. Hopefully, it will spill over into other areas as we role-model it, but that is secondary."

Errico sees the creation of a high-performing team as a survival strategy. "You know, from experience, the benefits of this way of working. You know that it is the best way to ensure that you will get the best out of your new team and replicate your past success. Why wouldn't you do it?"

Errico suggests that the leader's first order of business should be to figure out what will motivate people to work in the new way. What bothers them about the *status quo*? What would they like to change? What do they think would make them more effective as a team? Then, show them how following the high-performance, horizontal model will bring about the desired changes. Errico remembers vividly a past experience taking on a new role. The members of her new team expressed great frustration at the layers of bureaucracy that prevented them from gaining access to the company's senior leaders. Errico knocked down walls by inviting senior leaders to meetings of the HR team. She created opportunities for the team to engage in dialogue with managers at all levels. Her team members witnessed, from their leader, the effectiveness of high-performing principles, which then opened them up to the possibility of becoming high-performance players.

No question about it, this is a tough challenge. It is not always possible to cordon off an area of responsibility to make it an independent high-performance, horizontal zone. Company-wide performance systems, for one, typically reward individual rather than team performance. The challenge here is for the leader to find alternative ways to recognize and reward players for following the principles of high performance. Another difficulty: Interactions with "outsiders" may become strained, as they take a dim view of high performers' attempts to hold them accountable, assume greater decision-making responsibility, or engage in straight talk.

Challenge: Bringing on New Players

Gold watches for retiring employees were once hot items. Every year, companies awarded them by the dozens to employees who had grown up—and old—faithfully serving the same company. Today, the gold-watch market for retirees is in a slump. The Bureau of Labor Statistics reports that for the year ending in August 2006 overall U.S. voluntary turnover was 23.4%.[2] That means that nearly one in four employees departs for other pastures every year—and that does not include those who are given their walking papers. Add to that the number of internal transfers and the repercussions of mergers and acquisitions and it is obvious that churn is a major challenge for teams—and organizations. How can organizations maintain high performance in a revolving-door world?

One answer is to keep the revolving door from spinning out of control. Companies an exciting long-term strategy and business prospects, effective operations, and progressive human resource policies are likely to have less turnover than others. But even great organizations have not brought turnover to a standstill. After all, high-performing executives are a favorite target of headhunters.

We believe that turnover is a fact of life in the postindustrial business world, which puts increasing priority on answering the question: What is the best way to bring on new players and integrate them into the life of a high-performing organization?

Onboarding within a high-performing environment is especially challenging. Not surprisingly, newcomers tend to feel as though they are entering a brave new world in which all the old axioms that worked for them in hierarchical organizations are suddenly up for grabs.

Think about it: Alignment is not only about reconstituting the performance context—strategy, goals, roles, accountabilities, and protocols for decision making—but it is also about reshaping business relationships as well. The alignment process creates a powerful, shared experience in which leaders and players learn to show up "for real": to be candid, depersonalize, confront one another, and hold one another accountable.

Alignment is a hard-won accomplishment achieved in a number of ways: "looking in the mirror" at oneself and others on the team; receiving feedback on past behavior and contracting for future changes; and resolving tough, often long-standing contentious issues directly and within the new horizontal decision-making framework.

Following are four practical tips taken from great leaders who have successfully met the onboarding challenge.

Start at the Beginning

Onboarding begins with the interview process. Great leaders play it straight right from the start by letting candidates know what to expect. This is what Scott Edmonds does so well. In his initial contact with candidates for executive positions at Chico's, Edmonds explains the high-performance, horizontal model and the company's commitment to it. He tells applicants just how working at Chico's will differ from their past experience: that they will be held accountable by both their leaders and peers, they will be expected to deliver on commitments or explain why they cannot do so, and that a significant part of their compensation will be based on the quality of their teamwork. He then probes for "fit and feel."

Recall the discussion in Chapter 3 about the mindset of a great player, which includes thinking like a director, putting the team first and one's function second, embracing accountability, and being comfortable with discomfort. Use these attributes as a screen during the candidate-assessment process. To what extent does a candidate measure up? Does the candidate's background reveal clues to how successful he or she will be in the new environment? Question carefully. For example, ask a candidate what the biggest mistake he or she has made professionally is. If the answer comes back, "I'm an overachiever," or "My standards are too high," be wary. A candidate who substitutes disguised strengths for weaknesses may be unable to even make it up to the first rung of the accountability ladder.

Stay Close

Keep close to new hires. One way to do this is by putting in place a weekly feedback session to answer questions and address needs and concerns. Be sure to include new hires in their team's continuing reassessment and skill-development sessions. At Chico's, twice a year all employees who have joined the company in the preceding six months attend an off-site meeting devoted to continuing the horizontal integration process.

Role-Model

Role-modeling is probably the single most important influence on behavior. Years ago, a team of sociologists studied the behavior of freshly minted, straight-out-of-the-academy police officers. They left the police academy brimming with pride and enthusiasm, which quickly turned to cynicism once they joined the police force. The behavior role-modeled by supervisors and peers was decisive in their change of heart.

David Greenberg, senior vice president of HR for L'Oréal, knows the decisive effect of leader and peer behavior on a "new recruit." As he puts it, "When you join a team of 11 people and see them all role-modeling these behaviors, you quickly see how to do it. You see that everyone has a voice at the table, that disagreement is okay, that conflict is dealt with by depersonalizing. If someone isn't available when they should be or is marching in a different direction than was agreed on, you see them being held accountable. This sets up and makes clear what the expectation is."

Provide Mentors

Mars Incorporated has found mentoring to be extremely effective in bringing new hires into the high-performance fold. Each new team member is "adopted" by another player, who takes responsibility for the day-to-day explanation and reinforcement of high-performing behaviors.

In one organization we work in, a formal mentoring program is being structured in which senior leaders are paired with high-potential up-and-comers. Current leaders are provided with coaching and mentoring skills; future leaders are also provided with skills to get the best out of their leader-coaches—and themselves. While this program is not for new recruits, the approach is well worth considering, especially when the new hire is a senior-level player.

Bringing on new talent helps an organization regenerate itself. It is a way of importing new skills, perspectives, and energy. Harnessing these gifts early on is a challenge, especially in high-performing environments. Manage them effectively, and you should continue to achieve standout performance.

Challenge: Debunking Myths

Beneath the conscious pattern of human activity lies a realm of unexamined premises and assumptions that can exercise a kind of gravitational pull on decision making. Myths, sacred cows, implicit beliefs, stories—call them what you will—must be brought to the surface and critically examined.

In our work, we have encountered a number of myths that impede progress toward a high-performance culture and organization. Following are the worst offenders that we singled out for examination—and debunking.

Myth: Conflict Is Bad; It Should Be Avoided

Is conflict intrinsically bad? Most people think so. It is a myth that often has a deadly effect on an organization's health and success. Here is the truth about conflict: It is neither good nor bad; *it just is.*

True, conflict is destructive when it diverts energy from important activities or issues, polarizes groups, causes irresponsible or regrettable behavior such as personal attacks, or leads to stalemates rather than decisions. But the dynamic tension that results when executives go head to head can also be a source of great creativity, excitement, and even strength. This healthy tension can help an organization develop the muscle it needs to vanquish less-well-endowed competitors. Probing management disagreements can spur effective problem solving and be a boon to creative strategic and operational decision making. Sharing competing viewpoints shapes and sharpens action as it opens up thinking to new possibilities. Conflict can keep a company alive and flourishing.

Whether conflict works for or against an organization—shores it up or undermines its foundation—depends squarely on *how conflict is managed.*

The high-performance model, in both its structure and its approach to relationship building, is primed to turn conflict into healthy confrontation and both into business results.

Myth: Success Is Leadership Dependent

In the old, hierarchical order, success often hinged on the leader's ability to make the right calls. Most leaders today readily acknowledge the flaw in conceiving of leadership as a one-person show. Globalization, data overload and complexity, the rate of change, and the need for speed make old-fashioned, hierarchical leadership a museum piece.

On a rational level, high-performance, horizontal leadership makes sense, but psychologically it is hard for many leaders to part with the myth that to achieve commanding results they must be in command.

The old-fashioned leadership approach must be scuttled. The great awakening comes when leaders see the advantage of using their team to "multiply themselves." This awakening comes from strictly utilitarian considerations: Leveraging the leadership talent of your team works best.

Myth: Great Business Teams Are an American Idea that Cannot Be Exported

"Great business teams, as we have described them, are a uniquely American construct": Do not believe this myth. Our 25-plus years of consulting with teams all over the world have convinced us that teams have at least as much in common as they have differences.

The *raison d'être* of business organizations is to drive up results by satisfying market demand. To do this better than a competitor requires teams, at all levels, to be aligned around the five key factors: strategy, goals, roles, protocols, and interpersonal relationships. They must be equipped with the same skill sets. In short, the high-performance, horizontal model is universally applicable and effective—with minor modifications.

In previous chapters, we touched upon some of the cultural differences that companies need to consider when aligning global teams, and we pointed out the need to structure the alignment so that trouble areas receive the most emphasis.

No doubt about it, there are differences in the ways teams operate in the global environment. For example, outside the United States interpersonal relationships are often subject to a number of taboos. In some countries it is simply not acceptable to question or contradict your boss, so getting players to hold their leaders accountable is a significant challenge. Here the leader plays a crucial role in breaking through the cultural taboos that stand in the way of high performance.

Germany is touted to be a place where leaders command and control. A while ago, we were working with a group of German managers and their leader to improve their conflict-management skills. Prior to the initial session, our consultant took the leader aside and counseled him to encourage the team to give him candid, honest feedback. To the consultant's surprise, the leader readily agreed. "What's important," he told his team during the session, "is that we come out of here with a better sense of how we need to operate and how I can be a better leader."

This opened up the floodgates. For the first time, team members told their leader how much they resented the fact that decisions were handed to them as *faits accomplis*. They said they were tired of only being seen; they wanted to be heard. They told their leader that he needed to respect their contribution to the business.

The leader not only accepted their open criticism of him but thanked them for their candor. He promised to do better in the future, thereby paving the way for a new way of interacting with them.

America surely has no monopoly on great business teams. With the right leaders, players, and tools, such teams can flourish everywhere.

Challenge: Measuring Results

How do you measure greatness? The only answer we can give is that every team and every organization has its own sets of hard and soft metrics, which tell it that making the shift to the new model has been worth it.

For example, Cathy Burzik's top team at Applied Biosystems owned the goals for the company. There were about 20 of these goals, four or five in each of five categories: customer, innovation, execution, building a high-quality people organization, and making the numbers. The goals were scorecard-like—very measurable—so it was easy to tell whether or not the teams accomplished them. Achieving them determined the top team's compensation and the compensation of everyone in the company. At AB it was easy to judge the effectiveness of going horizontal.

At L'Oréal USA, Senior Vice President of HR David Greenberg and his team have agreed on and implemented what they term a "people P&L." Epstein describes this as "a simple set of metrics that allows us to gauge our progress in a variety of areas: employee retention, training and development, diversity, recruitment. It enables us to get past just the numbers and into action planning; when we see that we have missed a target, we will develop a plan to improve results."

To measure "softer" results, such as degree of engagement, each year Mars Incorporated asks its associates to complete a "Gallup 12Q" survey made up of 12 true-or-false statements, including: I know what is expected of me at work; at work I have the opportunity to do what I do best every day; the mission or purpose of my company makes me feel my job is important; and my supervisor is someone at work who seems to care about me as a person. President Paul Michaels says that the responses, along with the results of our reassessment surveys, give him a good idea of how high-performance oriented Mars' culture has become.

Revenue, profitability, and return—the *what* of results—are important indicators of the value of the high-performance, horizontal model. But so is the *how* by which you achieve them, which is why great leaders are attentive to both the hard and soft factors and insist on measuring both.

Challenge: When There Is No Support from the Top

Manuel Jessup, currently chief HR officer at Chico's, recalls his experience at a former company, where high-performing teams had been cascaded down from the top over a period of several years. The president and CEO of the division, as well as its group president, "lived and breathed" the high-performance ideas, according to Jessup. "It was the employer and division of choice in the area," he says. "We had no trouble recruiting and retaining talent. Creativity abounded; people felt free to take risks. Product innovations were made that still exist today. Sales and profits soared."

Then everything changed. The group president left, and the president and CEO of the division was no longer allowed to play by high-performance rules. "The new group president wasn't authentic," reflects Jessup. "He would go underground with a core team that made the decisions and drove the strategy. Previously, the division had thrived by working interdependently with the rest of the group; now, it was pushed aside and ignored."

To make things worse, disheartened by the turn of events, the president and CEO also left; and the division began to suffer from the implications of a hierarchical organization opposed to a horizontal team. "People began leaving in droves," Jessup recalls. "Sales and profits dropped; innovations stopped. The high-performing teams that we had created were disbanded. The numbers started to fall, and the damage was permanent."

Can a high-performing team constructively counterattack? The divisional answer is "yes," but it is not easy. Cathy Burzik states the challenge with considerable insight: "Any time the leader doesn't have high-performance training and the team does, there will be problems," she states. "The question is, 'Is the team strong enough to hold the leader accountable?' Will the players be able to tell the new leader that he or she has to become part of the team—another team member, in fact? Will they be strong enough to say, 'This is the way our company operates, and you have got to operate the same way. We want to see a change in you.' When the new leader is a command-and-control type, it's difficult to stand up for the high-performance way, but if you don't, it won't survive."

Is the leader capable of being swayed by results? If so, then think tactically about where in the organization high-performing teams have the highest likelihood of succeeding. Work with them, demonstrate results, and other areas will be lining up to get in on the action, as the following example demonstrates.

Vice President of Global HR for Wyeth Consumer Healthcare Ray Carson, Jr. and his team realized that alignment was key to the success of the business. Innovation was identified as a key priority and they received the green light to align the division's newly formed innovation teams. In addition, Carson asked several senior executives what they thought was the best way to improve the division's performance. Were there any areas in which alignment could significantly impact results? Which functions could benefit most? The most common response was "Sales and Marketing," so those were the other two areas selected to be aligned.

Challenge: Sustaining Momentum

We have spoken about the need to sustain high performance, but we want to flag it again here as a significant challenge, given all the forces at work in an organization—from strategic change to turnover—that can slow or even reverse momentum. In Chapter 5, we offered some suggestions: ending each meeting with a brief "How Are We Doing?" segment; having a process observer sit in on meetings and point out backsliding and failure to observe protocols; holding periodic formal reassessments; and, if necessary, recalibrating the team. All of these actions are important, but even more important is attitude.

As INTTRA's CEO, Ken Bloom, tells his employees, "If you think we are done, you are *done*." In other words, the *status quo* is the enemy of great teams and organizations. Every goal that is "done" should be a springboard to the next level of performance.

Periodic soul-searching is another ally of sustaining momentum. Here is former president of Applied Biosystems' Global Services Division Mike Schneider's version of looking inward: "When I find my results are starting to slip, I ask myself, 'What enabled me to achieve the success I've enjoyed the past two years? What is it that's missing?' I usually come to the realization that I've started to backslide. I've reverted to behavior that I engaged in two years ago; I'm not utilizing what I've learned."

Soul-searching and gathering together like-minded souls are an effective one-two combination for keeping energy up and momentum going.

Conclusion

Business leaders in every age are confronted with a unique set of challenges. Those that rise to the occasion build organizations that achieve standout performance and create enduring value.

Today's generation of leaders face great challenges, perhaps greater than any of their predecessors. Globalization, technology, fierce competition, the need for rapid innovation, dwindling natural resources, talent scarcity, and much more create a new set of demands and cross-pressures on today's organizations and those who lead them.

The leaders whom you have encountered in these pages understand that the old truisms of corporate success are no longer valid. They share a common set of assumptions about what it takes to achieve greatness in these revolutionary times, and they share a common set of solutions for meeting the seemingly intractable performance and value-creation challenges. They believe in—and are willing to stake their future and the future of their organization on—building a radically different organization, one that is horizontal in structure, that redefines the nature of leadership, and that is driven by great business teams that are aligned, accountable, and riveted on achieving an ever-higher measure of results.

Is the high-performance, horizontal organization worth the effort? The leaders we know think it is, in terms of both bottom-line results and the excitement that comes when an organization multiplies its effectiveness by tapping into everyone's brainpower.

Now that you have learned to crack the code for standout performance, why not start right away? What business issues are confronting you, your team, your organization? What will it take, now and going forward, to resolve them? What would greatness look like? Are you willing to hold up a mirror to your leadership behavior to begin the journey to high performance? Are you ultimately willing to authentically engage your team, so that you can "go there" together?

Notes

1. Lucier, Chuck, Steven Wheeler, and Rolf Habbel. "The Era of the Inclusive Leader," *strategy + business,* Issue 47, Summer 2007.
2. Nobscot Corporation, "Latest BLS Employer Turnover Rates for Year Ending August, 2006," www.nobscot.com/survey/index.cfm

Appendix A

Player–Centered Leadership

Great leaders know that there is no one "right way" to lead. They know how to vary their decision-making behavior depending on the skill level of each team member. They may *prescribe/direct,* telling players the what, where, when, and how of an issue. Or they may *coach/instruct,* de-emphasizing the how in favor of the *why.* They may choose to *collaborate/partner* with their teams. Or they may choose to *inspire/empower,* allowing team members to "run with the ball."

Here is a brief description of each of the four leadership behaviors:

Prescribing/Directing

Prescribing/Directing has always been the norm in hierarchical organizations: "Don't ask why, just do it," was a common refrain. In horizontal, matrix organizations, where managers often need to get results from those over whom they have no direct authority, the ability to *influence*—to persuade others to change their point of view and behavior so they are aligned with yours—is a critical skill.

That does not mean that a leader should never issue directions to a player. Directing can be about more than barking orders; it can be a helpful, mentoring behavior—if carried out in the right spirit and tone. Sometimes, it is obvious from the questions the player asks that he or she needs guidance or direction in order to carry out a task or make a decision. In other cases, the leader may suspect or recognize that the person's skills are not quite up to the assignment. In this case, the leader needs to test the person's capabilities with questions such as:

- What experience have you had working with _____?
- When you had a project similar to _____, what were the first steps you took to get it rolling? How would you begin to get this project going?
- When you put together task forces in the past, how did you decide who should be on the team? Who would you want on the team for this project?

The responses to these and other capability-testing questions tell the leader a great deal about the individual's ability to work independently and about the degree of direction that he or she will need.

Coaching/Instructing

Even in cases where players possess the ability and willingness to step up to increased responsibility, leaders must proceed cautiously. Before leaders can legitimately hold people accountable for solving problems, making decisions, and managing conflict, they must ratchet up the level of competency. By coaching players through tough issues, leaders help them develop the skills they will need to operate effectively on their own.

One key to effective coaching/instructing is to refuse to be drawn into the "content trap." Once a leader becomes entangled in the details of an issue, it is often hard to resist the temptation to start giving advice and offering solutions, which completely defeats the purpose of coaching. Here, there is an obvious parallel with the old saying, "Give a man a fish and you feed him for a day; teach him how to fish and you feed him for a lifetime." Give a player a solution and you enable that person to resolve a specific issue; teach a player how to arrive at solutions and you enable that person to resolve future issues.

Collaborating/Partnering

Many players are anxious about "trying their wings," even after considerable coaching. An astute leader recognizes this and shifts his or her behavior accordingly. Agreeing to collaborate along with the player or players in the resolution of the issue is often a good compromise. But before the leader commits to this arrangement, it is important to make clear the reasons he or she is going to be involved.

We recommend that the leader ask the following clarifying questions:

- Why do you believe that it is necessary for me to collaborate in the resolution of this issue?
- What is the value you see yourself bringing to the resolution of this issue?
- What value do you see me bringing?
- What do you need/want from me in order to make this collaboration work?
- What can I expect from you?
- Who will have the final say?

While collaborating in a problem-solving or decision-making session, the leader can take the opportunity to do some additional coaching, increasing the skills and confidence level of those involved.

Inspiring/Empowering

Inspiring/Empowering requires the highest level of trust. When a leader empowers others, he or she hands over the reins, in one area at least, to one or more members of the team. They are on their own, fully accountable—and, hopefully, fully equipped—to take action.

Once again, it is the responsibility of the leader to make sure that those who will be held accountable for results are set up for success and not failure. Before empowering others, the leader needs to ask:

- Do they have all the information, or access to the information sources, that they will need to resolve this issue?

- Do they have the resources, such as headcount, budget, and space, with which to carry out their assignment?
- Do they have all the tools they will need, including hardware, software, and printed materials?
- Have they forged, or have I forged for them, relationships with colleagues whose help they may need during the project?

Homing in on the Leadership Needs of Your Players

Leaders must adjust their behaviors to the needs of their players. Diagnosing those needs—and determining which leadership behavior to adopt—entails analyzing two factors:

ENGAGEMENT: An individual's commitment to being a team player; his or her willingness to take ownership of and be held accountable for the team's success; his or her intention to embrace the attributes of high-performing teams.

SKILLS: The knowledge and skills an individual brings to a goal or task; education, experience, and/or ability; the individual's appropriate utilization of his or her technical/leadership, interpersonal, and strategic skills in the context of meeting performance targets.

Depending on the degree to which they are engaged and skilled, players will fall into one of four major categories.

- low level of engagement and/or skill set
- moderately low level of engagement and/or skill set
- moderately high level of engagement and/or skill set
- high level of engagement and skill set

Adjusting Leader Behavior to Player Needs

We recommend that leaders use the following guidelines to determine the behavior to use when working with each kind of player, depicted in Figure A.1.

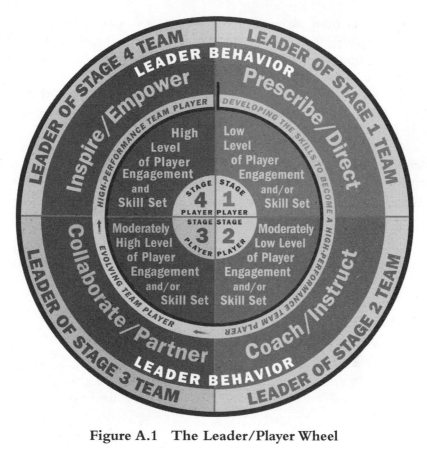

Figure A.1 The Leader/Player Wheel

Player Engagement and Skill Stages	Recommended Leader Behavior
Stage 1—Low level of engagement and/or skill set	Stage 1—Prescribe/Direct
Stage 2 – Moderately low level of engagement and/or skill set	Stage 2—Coach/Instruct
Stage 3 – Moderately high level of engagement and/or skill set	Stage 3—Collaborate/Partner
Stage 4—High level of engagement and skill set	Stage 4 – Inspire/Empower

As an individual progresses from a "Low level of engagement and/or skill set" (Stage 1) to a "Moderately high level of engagement and/or skill set" (Stage 3), the leader needs to reduce the amount of direction and increase the amount of support.

When a player reaches a "High level of engagement and skill set" (Stage 4), the leader decreases the amount of both directive and supportive behavior.

The result: A Stage 4 leader allows increased delegation and empowerment for task completion, which promotes higher levels of ownership and accountability. This behavior is seen as an indication of trust and increased levels of confidence and commitment.

Appendix B
The Skills of a Great Team Member

The Primacy of Influence

In today's matrixed organizations and on the cross-functional teams that predominate in them, traditional power-based leader-subordinate relationships are evolving to a more nuanced set of relationships between individuals who have little or no authority over one another. In the world of horizontal, rather than hierarchical, relationships, every team member needs the skills to influence and persuade colleagues over whom he or she has no direct control.

Baseline Capabilities

To be an effective influencer requires a keen ability both to assess where others stand vis-à-vis you and your agenda and to know your own style.

Assessing Where Others Stand

One of the key capabilities of a leader is the ability to develop "framing strategies" for dealing with his or her colleagues. In other words, to home

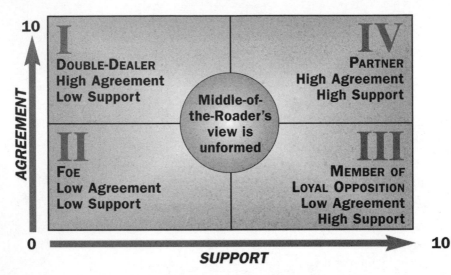

Figure B.1   Matrix for Framing Strategies

in on a particular situation, assess each player in terms of the degree of their agreement and support for the issue on the table, and then develop a strategy for winning them over.

Figure B.1 provides a key to developing framing strategies. It depicts people in terms of two variables: the degree to which they agree with you and the amount of support they are willing to give you. Agreement is represented by the vertical axis, with "0" indicating total lack of agreement and "10" complete agreement. Support, on the horizontal axis, ranges from "0"—no support whatsoever—to "10"—total, unreserved support.

Do not attempt to bring a colleague around to your point of view unless you have a clear answer to two questions. First: To what extent does the individual agree with your mission? In other words, does the person share the same fundamental goals as you, and is he or she working toward the same end? Second: To what extent can you count on this person as a supporter?

Once you have the answers to these questions, you can begin to outline a strategy for dealing with the individual in question. The Matrix for Framing Strategies presents the range of available options, given the two crucial dimensions of agreement and support.

The Double Dealers described in Quadrant I agree with you at the business-concept level but for some reason decide to withhold their support. Do not waste time presenting a business case to these people: You are preaching to the converted. The key challenge here is to win their support. Suggestion: Focus on listening to their concerns, encouraging them to speak candidly, and working to build trust between you.

The Foes in Quadrant II are the immovable forces in the work environment. They neither agree with your goals, nor are they among your supporters. Influencing foes can be a Herculean task. Expect foes to be locked into going-in stories that prevent them from engaging authentically. Until you understand what beliefs are keeping them from taking an objective view, you will be unable to exercise any influence over them. Suggestion: Encourage candor, story-sharing, and the forging of new agreements for moving ahead.

The Members of the Loyal Opposition in Quadrant III support you while disagreeing with your point of view. They trust you but are at odds with your approach to an issue. With this group, your strategy must be the polar opposite of that used with the Double Dealers. Suggestion: Present a strong business case, as objectively as possible, to turn your colleagues around.

The remaining two groups—the Partners in Quadrant IV and the Middle-of-the-Roaders in the center—present opportunities. The former group supports you and agrees with you. Having them in your corner is an excellent way to demonstrate to others the value of your ideas. The Partners can have a positive influence on others, especially the Middle-of-the-Roaders. These individuals, who have yet to form an opinion, can be transformed into strong supporters if you can identify their concerns and develop a plan to address them. Suggestions: Enlist the aid of Partners. Engage in candid dialogue with the Middle-of-the-Roaders and you will likely transform them into partners.

Assessing Where YOU Stand

The second baseline capability that is key to influencing others is an understanding of how *you* deal with conflict. This entails being crystal clear on where you stand in terms of two personality dimensions: assertiveness and cooperativeness.

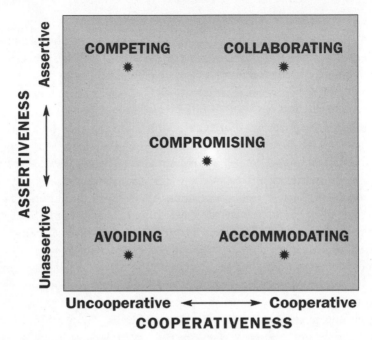

Figure B.2   The Thomas–Kilmann Conflict Mode Instrument

Assertiveness is the extent to which a person attempts to satisfy his or her own needs. We have already gone into considerable detail about the importance of knowing where your behavior falls on the continuum from nonassertive to assertive to aggressive. *Cooperativeness* is the extent to which an individual attempts to satisfy another person's needs. When you look at these two basic dimensions of behavior in conjunction with one another and assess the degree of balance that exists between the concern for one-self and for others, it becomes possible to identify five distinct methods that people employ when dealing with conflict.

Figure B.2, The Thomas–Kilmann Conflict Mode Instrument[1], is a graphic representation of these five methods.

Thomas and Kilmann define each method as follows:

- *Competing* implies being assertive and uncooperative. An individual who chooses this method is more interested in pursuing his or her own concerns at the expense of others. This individual uses whatever power is necessary to win. When a person competes, he or she defends a position at all costs.

- *Accommodating* entails being unassertive and cooperative. This method, which is the opposite of competing, implies self-sacrifice. The accommodating individual chooses to neglect his or her own concerns in order to satisfy the concerns of others. This method requires giving in to another's point of view even when you prefer not to.

- *Avoiding* is being unassertive and uncooperative. An individual using this method merely chooses not to take action at this time, either for him- or herself or for others. As a result, the conflict remains unaddressed. The avoidance behavior might take the form of sidestepping the discussion of an issue, postponing it, or withdrawing from what the individual perceives as a threatening situation.

- *Compromising* involves being square in the middle in terms of both assertiveness and cooperativeness. This method is often expedient. Both parties seek to quickly arrive at some middle ground—splitting the difference, in a sense. The end result might be a solution that is mutually acceptable yet only partially satisfying to each side.

- *Collaborating* means being both assertive and cooperative. Collaborating requires that both sides be willing to work together to find a solution that fully satisfies the concerns of each. It involves an in-depth exploration of differences in order to learn from each other's insights.

With these methods in mind, take a few moments to decide where on the model your workplace behavior generally falls. Then, think about the reaction this behavior provokes in others—and the effect it has on your ability to work harmoniously with them:

- Are you often kept in the dark because people would rather keep their opinions to themselves than deal with your hard-nosed attitude?
- Would your colleagues respond more positively to your suggestions if you were less aggressive and more cooperative?
- Are your needs frequently unmet, either because you cannot assert yourself or because you refuse to budge from your position?
- Do you often feel like a doormat because you would rather accommodate others than assert yourself?
- Do you usually seek a middle-of-the-road solution, a compromise, in order to put an end to dissention?

■ Are you able to assert yourself without appearing uncooperative? In other words, are you a collaborative individual, whom everyone wants on their team?

The answer to the last question in the sequence separates superior conflict managers from the rest of the lot. If your answer was "yes," you are indeed rare. Very few people are able, without training, to cooperate without giving in, to assert themselves without stepping on toes—in short, to honor others' needs without sacrificing their own.

The two baseline capabilities that we just described are essential tools in all conflict situations. But every conflict situation in the workplace poses unique challenges and, therefore, requires situation-specific skills. Let us examine these skills in some detail.

Which Skills, When?

Consider the following three distinct conflict situations and the repertoire of skills each requires:

■ *When another person's needs are pressing . . . you need active listening skills.*[2]
■ *When your needs are pressing . . . you need assertion skills.*
■ *When both people's needs are pressing . . . you need conflict management skills.*

Let's examine the first scenario: When another person comes to you and expresses a concern that needs to be resolved.

I. Using Active Listening Skills

Active listening is easier said than done. We find it difficult to listen to others for a number of reasons.

Studies have shown that a human being can think five times faster than he or she can speak. This simple fact accounts for much of the difficulty we have listening to others. While the speaker struggles to get the words out, our mind races ahead. During the lag time we may become impatient, angry, bored, or distracted. As a result, we develop a coping strategy. We either tune them out or attempt to complete the thought for them.

Being an attentive listener is a challenge for several other reasons:

- *It is not natural.* The natural human response is to react from one's sense of need. It is part of our basic survival instinct to put our own needs first, and listening to those of others is not our first priority.
- *Our biases influence our reactions.* Our perceptions have been molded by a lifetime of experience—both positive and negative. As a result, we have certain going-in stories about men who have long hair, women who wear mini-skirts, representatives of certain ethnic groups, and people who are much older or much younger than we. These and other deep-seated biases cause us to "filter" speakers' messages: We hear what people say in a different light, depending on the preconceived notions we have of them.
- *We are always in our own conversation.* Because our brain works so quickly and constantly, we are always noticing and evaluating what comes into our awareness. It is as if another person were inside our head, whispering, "I like this," or "I disagree with that," or "What should we have for dinner tonight?" Sometimes our conversation with our inner person becomes so engaging that it is hard to stay focused on what a speaker is trying to convey to us.
- *We have a preprogrammed style.* Years of experience and learning have caused us to develop habitual ways of responding to the world around us. Add to this the impact of personality and genetics, and you find that each of us tends to react to certain situations in our own pre-programmed fashion. When confronted with another person's needs, especially if that person is in a heightened emotional state, one individual might be too embarrassed to respond, another might be offended, yet another might feel compelled to offer advice or comfort. Whatever our typical response is, it is difficult to make a conscious choice about how to behave in such a situation.

Listening: Behaviors to Avoid   Not focusing on those who come to us with a concern can bruise egos, but we add insult to injury by continually interrupting. Yet, many of us feel compelled to interject our own reaction or opinion into another's story. We do this for various reasons: We are used to participating in a dialogue, not listening to a monologue; we think the speaker expects us to offer, if not a solution, at least an expression of sympathy; we want to cut short the conversation before it becomes a protracted saga. Such "roadblock responses" cause a barrier to go up between us and the speaker.

Roadblock responses fall into three categories:

- *Sending solutions* impedes effective communication. In our desire to help someone—or shortcut the conversation—we may come in too rapidly with our own opinion. This can be discouraging to the speaker. After all, he or she may be in search of a sounding board, not a solution. It also subtly shifts the focus from the speaker and puts it on *me*.
- *Evaluating* is another way in which to alienate someone who is looking for a listener. In our attempt to help the speaker or speed up the process, we turn him or her off by using judgmental remarks, which signal agreement, lack of agreement, skepticism, and the like. These remarks may provoke defensive behavior from the speaker; communication becomes tense or completely closed off; and the speaker typically leaves with a feeling of dissatisfaction and discomfort.
- *Withdrawing* is another deadly response. When we do not have time to listen, are not interested, or are uncomfortable with the message we are hearing, we consciously or subconsciously cut ourselves off or withdraw from the conversation. We may become totally unresponsive, or we may change the subject to one that better suits us.

All of these responses block, either temporarily or permanently, the transmission of the speaker's message. They tend to lower the speaker's self-esteem, cause the speaker to become either resistant or defensive, diminish his or her sense of responsibility, convey hidden messages, and, worst of all, keep the speaker from finding a solution to a troublesome problem.

Active Listening: Behaviors and Techniques[3]   Whenever a person expresses a concern or need, you, the listener, need to be aware of two things: the content of the message and the emotion behind it. The content element of the message is the proverbial tip of the iceberg. The most significant part of the message is to be found below the surface: the speaker's underlying feelings about the issue at hand. When someone comes to you with an issue, you want to get past the tip and into the core as quickly as possible. Active Listening skills are designed to help penetrate to the depths.

Active Listening is not limited to the ears. It involves the whole body—and the brain. There are five very effective Active Listening techniques that can improve your listening skills—and assure the speaker that he or she has an attentive, nonjudgmental audience.

1. Attending Behavior.

By demonstrating attending behavior, a listener conveys the message that he or she is "all ears": ready to focus completely on what the speaker has to say. Here is a first-step suggestion that many executives overlook: Be sure that your conversation takes place in a suitable environment: private, nonthreatening, without distractions and without physical barriers between the parties. Think about it: If you entered your boss's office for a "moment of truth" meeting, what would make you more comfortable? If you were separated from him or her by a desk the size of Rhode Island or if the two of you were sitting around a coffee table?

Body language speaks volumes, as we all know, and is an important way in which a listener demonstrates attentiveness. Body position, facial expression, and gestures such as head nodding and hand movements provide cues that you are tuned in—or out.

The SOLER Model shown in Figure B.3 is a quick reference that can help listeners remember the key points of Attending Behavior.

> **S** – Sit (or stand) squarely
> **O** – Open posture
> **L** – Lean forward
> **E** – Eye contact
> **R** – Relaxed posture/respect other

Figure B.3　The SOLER Model of Attending Behavior

These nonverbal behaviors have a tremendous impact on the effectiveness of communication. Together with tone of voice—volume, pitch, intensity, inflection—they are responsible for the lion's share of what people take away from an interaction. Studies show that the message retained after an interpersonal exchange is derived 55% from nonverbal behavior, 35% from tone, and only 7% from words.

2. Passive Listening.

Passive listening as an Active Listening Skill? Is this just another oxymoron? It makes perfect sense, however, when you realize that you need to *actively listen passively*. Simply remaining silent and allowing the speaker to talk sounds easy, but it is often a challenge, as the widespread tendency to engage in roadblock responses demonstrates. But, as difficult as it is to maintain, a period of silence is useful because it allows the speaker time to express, without interruption, his or her thought. During this time, the listener may choose to:

- attend to the speaker by just listening and giving eye contact
- observe the speaker's eyes, facial expressions, posture, and gestures to receive additional insight
- think about what the speaker is saying and feeling

This behavior demonstrates, without the listener having to verbalize, that he or she is totally involved in the needs of the speaker.

3. "Say more" responses.

Say more responses are phases that encourage the speaker to tell you more about his or her ideas and feelings. They can be neutral statements such as, "Really," "Uh huh," and "Oh?" or more direct invitations to continue, such as "Tell me more," "Go ahead," and "Would you like to talk about it?" Say more responses should not communicate any of the listener's own judgments, thoughts, or feelings. Rather, the responses are meant to convey empathy—to let the speaker know that you are putting yourself in his or her shoes to better understand his or her sense of reality.

4. Paraphrasing.

Paraphrasing means repeating back to the speaker, in your own words, you understanding of what he or she has just told you. "Mirroring" is another word for this technique, which eliminates the potential for misunderstanding.

When paraphrasing, focus on the *content* of the message, not the emotion behind it. Try to capture, as concisely as possible, *what* the speaker has said. Then, ask the speaker to confirm that your interpretation of the message is correct.

Here are some formulations you can use when paraphrasing:

"It sounds like . . ."
"So, what you're saying is . . ."
"It seems to me that you . . ."
"Let me see if I understand you correctly . . ."

"When you say _____, do you mean _____?"

5. Decoding and feeding back feelings.

Once you are sure you understand the *what* of the message, it is time to search for the *why*: to decode the message and then reflect back the thoughts and feelings that you believe the speaker is sharing. This is often very difficult to do, because when people speak to one another, especially about charged issues, they often encode the message rather than "let it all hang out." Age, sex, cultural differences, educational differences, and belief systems of both the speaker and listener are common filters that prevent speakers from delivering their messages clearly and concisely. Also, speakers often disguise their real intentions for fear of hurting others or using words inappropriately. As a result, the listener may only be able to partially decode the message.

To complicate the process further, just as the speaker may encode inaccurately, so may the listener decode inaccurately as a result of his or her own filtering system.

As with paraphrasing, it is helpful to remember that the goal of decoding and feeding back is to communicate to the speaker your understanding of the subtext of his or her message and your acceptance of his or her reality. By providing the speaker with a restatement or reworking of the emotional message, you indicate whether or not you "got it." If the restatement is accurate, the speaker will be encouraged to go on. If the restatement is not correct, the speaker receives the signal to clarity the message more accurately.

When a person transmits a message about emotions, sometimes what is *not* spoken reveals more than what is. True feelings are often revealed more by a gesture, a facial expression, or the tone or volume of voice than by the words. When decoding it is important to be receptive to both verbal and nonverbal clues.

Here are some examples of phrases you can use when feeding back to a speaker the emotions you have decoded during your Active Listening:

"That really ANNOYED you."
"You're NERVOUS."
"You seem FRUSTRATED."
"It sounds like you're CONFUSED about ..."
"You look SURPRISED."

Moving from Listening to Action   Active Listening is a tool used to defuse a person's emotions. Giving the person an opportunity to present his or her case without interruption immediately takes the edge off the situation. If the individual was expecting an argument or even a logical rebuttal, he or she will be pleasantly surprised—and encouraged to be less defensive and more cooperative. By analyzing, then feeding back, the content and emotion that come through to you, you convey to the speaker your interest in and empathy for his or her concern. Before you know it, a potential adversary has been turned into a partner.

Once both parties are clear about the message being sent, the listener, through his or her subsequent behavior, can help the speaker to take ownership and responsibility for the issue and, eventually, to find a solution. Once the facts have been uncovered, the listener can question, advise, and use logical arguments or praise to get the speaker thinking about solutions. Steering the speaker toward an action plan to resolve the issue is not only appropriate, but is also desirable at this point in the interaction.

II. Using Assertion Skills

In the second scenario—when *your* needs are pressing—Assertion Skills are the solution. The trick here is maintaining that delicate balance between standing up for what you value and believe while respecting the needs or others.

The nonassertive individual, in effect, says, "I've got needs and so do you, but I'm not telling you what mine are. And if you don't guess them, I'm going to hold it against you." The nonassertive individual is like a smoldering volcano, waiting to erupt. At the other extreme, the aggressive individual proceeds on the basis that, "I've got needs and, at best, so do you, but mine count more." This is the schoolyard bully in business attire.

It is crucial to recognize the proper boundaries for each of the three behaviors on the continuum. Boundaries may be either physical or psychological. *Physical* boundaries refer to variables that are tangible and quantifiable. If another person's behavior costs you money or wastes your time, your physical boundaries have been invaded. *Psychological* boundaries refer to variables that are intangible and more difficult to quantify. They may include people trying to control you, make decisions for you, second-guess your decisions, go over your head to your boss with their issues, and so on.

People who are nonassertive, for example, must learn how to protect their boundaries—whether physical or psychological—and express their agenda without crossing the line to aggression. The aggressive individual, by contrast, must learn not to violate the boundaries of others.

As we stressed earlier, each behavior on the continuum has payoffs, and each exacts a price. For the nonassertive executive, the payoff is avoiding arguments and coming across as a team player. But the price is steep in terms of unmet needs and diluted effectiveness. Aggressive executives tend to get their way and benefit from the charisma of *machismo*. They pay the price, however, in alienating others, closing down input and feedback, and failing to gain commitment, especially in the new knowledge-based organization.

Being assertive forces compromise and takes patience and time, but it has all the benefits of a win–win approach.

Skills for the Art of Assertion　The vice president of marketing for a New York cosmetics giant was not having much fun. She was hard working, hard driving, and deeply committed to getting results. But her department was plagued by turnover and, increasingly, her peers on the senior management team ran the other way rather than face the possibility of being assigned to a project or task force with her. She did not work well cross-functionally, and she became more and more isolated. As talented as she was, her manager felt that she was becoming a liability. Either she "dialed down" her behavior or she faced being jettisoned.

In another case, the vice president of operations in a Midwest manufacturing organization occupied the other extreme. He was the ultimate nice guy. He was a good delegator but felt uncomfortable holding his employees accountable for results. He found it difficult to be directive and was a poor coach. His people exhibited little sense of urgency, and work fell between the cracks. His story was, "I want to respect my people." Clearly, this vice president's behavior had to be "dialed up" to improve his level of play.

Ms. Dial Down and Mr. Dial Up clearly required coaching. Ms. Dial Down needed to become a better listener and improve her ability to understand resistance and deal with it without creating enemies. Mr. Dial Up had to become more assertive and more willing to confront. Each had to learn the skills that would enable them to move toward the mid-point of assertion. These include: Persistence, Sidestepping, Straight Talk, and the Three-Part "I" Response.

Let us take a closer look at each of these skills and how they can help you move your behavior along the continuum.

1. Persistence.

How do you make it clear to someone who is trying to invade your boundaries that their behavior is unacceptable? By being persistent. By repeating the same response, over and over, until they get the point. For example, you might keep saying, "I have a concern about what you just said."

This is a very tricky technique because it is designed to avoid engagement. It is often difficult to carry out with someone close to you. It works best with people with whom you are not trying to cultivate lasting relationships, such as salespeople, contribution seekers, telemarketers, and so on. No matter whom you attempt to use it on, be polite and gracious, but do not allow them to trap you into giving reasons or explaining why you must say "no." Just sound like a broken record!

2. Sidestepping.

Use this technique when you want to end a discussion or avoid an argument. When people begin to debate any subject about which they have strong feelings, emotions quickly take over. Remember, what is said in the heat of the moment cannot be taken back and can seriously impair a relationship. Whether in the workplace or outside, there are times when it behooves you to "dial down" your response. Sidestepping can help you emerge gracefully from a potentially explosive situation.

When you sidestep, you acknowledge that the other person may have a good point. You simply say, "You may be right" or "That's certainly a possibility," and refuse to argue any further. Saying these words does not mean you are admitting that you are wrong or that you agree with the other person, but it does defuse the situation.

3. Straight talk.

Straight Talk is a powerful, direct, and open means of communicating your wants and needs. Use it when you want to modify another person's behavior in order to get your needs met. In order to make sure the other person understands what you are saying in Straight Talk, be specific and concise. Put your statement into the following format:

I want/need . . . . *because* . . . .

For example, "I want you to supply me with the financial data before noon because I have to have my report completed by 5 PM." Or, "I need you to approve the new package design by the end of the week, because it's going into production on Monday."

Combining your request with a reason conveys the idea that you respect the other person enough to feel that he or she deserves an explanation. It prevents you from being perceived as aggressive. It turns what may have been construed as a command into a request, making people more willing to honor it. It is an excellent way to raise the other person's level of cooperativeness.

Unfortunately, many people will not take no for an answer or tune out information that is not welcome. With such individuals, both Sidestepping and Straight Talk may have to be combined with Persistence in order to get the point across.

4. The three-part "I" response.

This technique is the most powerful—and the most difficult—of the assertiveness techniques. It is used when you are not getting what you want or when you are getting what you do not want. It is designed to protect your boundaries and to change others' behaviors. Unlike simple Persistence, which is most useful when you are not terribly concerned about alienating the individual, you will want to use this technique with people whom you know well and with whom you have a long-standing, important relationship.

The Three-Part "I" message is comprised of three distinct parts:

| A description of the troublesome behavior | + | The disclosure of your feelings about the behavior | + | The effect it has on you |

When you deliver the message, it is most effective if you use the following formulation:

When you . . .   +   I feel . . .   +   because . . .

For example, "*When you* don't give me the financial data on time, *I feel* nervous and pressured *because* I still have to complete my report by the deadline." Or, "*When you* aren't available to approve a design, *I feel* frustrated *because* I can't move the project to the next stage."

The "I" part of the message is especially important. A "you" message blames the other party and is likely to trigger defensive behavior. An "I" message is not likely to be viewed as a personal attack the way a "you" message is. By using the "I" formulation, the speaker accepts full responsibility for his or her reaction to the behavior.

When you give others the opportunity to examine their own behaviors in a nonthreatening atmosphere, they tend to be more willing to change their behaviors to meet your needs. And that, after all, is your goal when you assert yourself.

A particularly powerful way to assert yourself when someone has violated your boundaries is to combine a Three-Part "I" Response with Straight Talk. The "I" message lets the other person know that you have an issue with his or her behavior and explains, clearly and in a depersonalized way, what that issue is. The Straight Talk communicates the change in behavior that you would like to see the person make going forward.

For example: "When you don't give me the financial data on time, I feel nervous and pressured because I still have to complete my report by the deadline. I want you to supply me with the financial data before noon because I have to have my report completed by 5 PM." Or, "When you aren't available to approve a design, I feel frustrated because I can't move the project to the next stage. I need you to approve the new package design by the end of the week, because it's going into production on Monday."

Assertiveness Cannot Hurt Many team members—especially the junior ones—fear that by being assertive they will alienate their superiors. They do not want to come across as pushy, egotistical, or lacking in respect for those with more experience. They worry that their assertiveness will be perceived as aggressiveness. Remember: Becoming assertive is one of the best ways to gain the respect of your peers and of senior management.

When you refuse to allow others—no matter what their level or experience—to walk over you, you establish yourself as a force to be reckoned with. By asserting yourself, you demonstrate your commitment to the success of the team. People recognize that you are engaged—in the game and willing to play for the high stakes. By refusing to allow others to ignore your needs, you ensure that you will not be ignored.

III. Using Conflict-Management Skills

Whenever two people have needs that are in opposition, and each is determined to prevail, defusing the situation requires the full range of conflict-management skills.

In every conflict situation, there are four options available for dealing with it:

1. Play the victim: say nothing, act powerless, and complain.
2. Leave: physically remove oneself from involvement.
3. Change oneself: move off one's position; shift one's view of the other party; "let it go."
4. Confront: address the issue openly, candidly, and objectively; communicate with the other party.

Option 1 is never viable. Playing the victim generally exacerbates a situation by sweeping conflict under the carpet. It causes hard feeling and delays the inevitable. The second option is often unavailable. Besides, conflict is a given and you better learn to deal with it here and now. Changing yourself is fine, but do not count on being able to do it. The question is: What price are you willing to pay?

This leaves confronting as the most effective way to resolve issues without igniting thermonuclear war. We recommend using an overall strategy for Confronting, which we call "The Four C's" approach.

The Four C's for Confronting   The Four C's that make up this strategy are:

1. *Connecting*: Establishing a rapport with the other party by (a) addressing the issue between you openly and candidly and (b) asserting yourself.
2. *Clarifying*: Seeking to understand by (a) Active Listening and (b) exploring all points of view.
3. *Confirming*: Reaching mutual agreement as to what each party wants and needs and establishing your willingness to collaborate.
4. *Contracting*: Negotiating agreements for future interaction.

While carrying out this conflict-resolution strategy, you will be using some of the techniques mentioned previously: assessing your style and your colleagues' methods of dealing with conflict, Active Listening skills, and Assertiveness Training.

Let us discuss each element of the confronting strategy in more detail:

1. *Connecting.*
Before attempting to connect with another person—to establish a rapport that is conducive to discussing your mutual needs—always check with the person to determine the best time and place to have your discussion. Do not forget Attending Behavior: Make sure you have privacy, will not be interrupted, are in a neutral, nonthreatening environment, have scheduled enough time to cover all the salient points, and that both of you have had enough time to prepare for your meeting.

Finding the right words to begin a potentially adversarial discussion can be difficult. We suggest using *Partnering Phrases,* which convey the idea that you are ready to address the issue candidly and objectively, and that you are serious about resolving it. For example:

- "I have some concerns about the way we are making decisions that I'd like to explore with you."
- "I have an issue with your attendance, and we can't afford to let this go unresolved."
- "We seem to have some fundamental differences about how to market the new product, and I'd like to address these with you."
- "I am having some difficulties with the way you are managing the IT project. They're really going to get in the way if we don't deal with them."
- "I'm uncomfortable with your approach to performance reviews, and I want to work my concerns out with you."

2. *Clarifying.*

Clarifying is a critical step in conflict management. Until both parties are clear about one another's issue, it is impossible to negotiate, or Contract, a mutually satisfying agreement. This is the ideal place to begin using your Active Listening skills to encourage the other party to open up about the real issues he or she has. Assertion skills will also help you describe the behaviors you are concerned about and the reasons you find them troubling.

Once again, choosing the right words is crucial. Try these Clarifying phrases:

- "Let's take a minute to clarify what we hear each other saying about the way we've been making decisions."
- "It's important for me to understand where you're coming from. What do I need to know to understand what's been happening with your attendance?"
- "Let's define our key concerns regarding marketing the new product. How about you expressing your concerns first, since they are important for me to understand."
- "Regarding the IT project, what feedback do you have for me about anything I've been doing to contribute to the situation?"
- "I want to know what you think. What is your point of view on performance reviews?"

3. *Confirming.*

Confirming entails summing up the facts: restating the issues to ensure that nothing has been misunderstood or omitted during your discussion. Equally important is a summary of the emotional progress that has been made: the commitment that you have both made to finding a mutually agreeable solution. Although at this point both parties are usually eager to move to action, investing a few additional minutes in Confirming will make the next step much easier.

Here are Confirming statements that executives have found useful:

- "Is there anything we missed that needs to be discussed regarding the marketing strategy?"
- "Here's my understanding of our differences and where we are right now on the issue of the IT project."
- "Do you have any other concerns about our performance reviews?"
- "I really appreciate your willingness to work through this issue with me."
- "I'm optimistic that we can find a win-win solution here."

4. *Contracting.*

Contracting is the final stage in managing conflict by confronting. It entails finding the win-win solution that both parties have committed to. At this point, one of the most effective tools available to executives is the combination of the Three-Part "I" Response and Straight Talk that we recommended as a way of asserting yourself.

Let us take the example of two IT executives responsible for the rollout of an ERP system. In the past two weeks, Deborah, the project manager, has authorized overtime to keep the project on schedule. Sam, her boss, has just learned about this from another manager. Sam's combination Three-Part "I" Response and Straight Talk might sound something like this:

"Deborah, when you authorize overtime without telling me, you put me in a difficult situation. I'm the one who's responsible for staying on budget, and if there are any cost overruns I'm the one who'll have to explain them. From now on, I need you to come to me before authorizing any overtime on the ERP rollout."

At this point, Deborah is likely to retort with an explanation of her behavior, such as: "You were away for the weekend; you said you couldn't be reached; and I had to make the call. I figured because you didn't give me your phone number, you didn't want me to bother you. If you want to make the decisions, I have to be able to get in touch with you."

Touché! Now Deborah is the one asserting herself, making it clear that she, too, has needs. The negotiation will now proceed, back and forth, until both Sam's and Deborah's needs are met. If Sam is not willing to give up his privacy by leaving a phone number, maybe he will agree to call Deborah for a daily update the next time he goes away. Or he may decide to give Deborah more leeway, arranging for her to authorize overtime up to a certain number of hours without his approval.

Some useful Contracting phrases are:

- "I think the whole team needs to be involved in budget decisions. What do you think?"
- "Having you work four 10-hour days doesn't work for me, but having you come in at 10 AM and work until 6 PM would. Would that work for you?"
- "Let's plan some practical next steps to develop the marketing plan together."
- "One thing we can do to move the IT project ahead is …"
- "What would you prefer that I do differently in the future regarding the way I conduct my performance reviews?"

Notes

1. This two-dimensional model of conflict-handling behavior is adapted from "Conflict and Conflict Management" by Kenneth Thomas in *The Handbook of Industrial and Organizational Psychology,* edited by Marvin Dunnette. Rand McNally, Chicago, 1976.
2. In the Appendix of Leader Effectiveness Training: LET, (p. 272), Thomas Gordon explains the origin of *Active Listening*: "The term 'Active Listening' was first suggested to me by Richard Farson. However, the technique itself is derived from the work of Carl Rogers and his psychology students, then at Ohio State University. At that time it was labeled 'reflection of feelings.'"
3. Both the Active Listening techniques outlined here and the Assertion Skills discussed later in this Appendix are not original with Guttman Development Strategies, Inc. Because they have been used by many others, for many years, we are unable to trace them with certainty to their originators.

Index